Mexico

In 2017 it was announced that a *tzompantli*, a tower of skulls, had been discovered during excavations at the Templo Mayor in Mexico City's historic centre. These towers were known to have existed from historic sources, but no examples had previously been found. The orderly rows of empty skulls are a horrific spectacle, but the practice of human sacrifice – we are reminded by Juan Villoro in the opening article of this issue – was part of a cosmology and shared system of values in which life was renewed through death. But what about the levels of violence in modern Mexico? The country is 'one big necropolis, seeded everywhere with contemporary skulls', in which eleven women are killed every day. Quite apart from the numbers, what is shocking is the level of impunity: 90 per cent of cases of femicide remain unsolved. Women themselves are leading the fight against the violence, to cries of 'we want to stay alive', presenting themselves as the only true opposition to the government, because, in spite of his rhetoric about 'hugs not bullets', the populist left-wing president Andrés Manuel López Obrador is going down the well-trodden path of Mexican politics and imposing solutions rather than listening to what people actually want. This is a familiar tale for the country's ethnolinguistic minorities, who are often on the receiving end of unsolicited policies and megaprojects, one such being the emblematic Tren Maya currently under construction in the jungle. The thinking behind the project is that it will bring 'progress' to the south-east of the country – although the people who live there have never been consulted on what exactly that might mean. It is too often forgotten that the Maya, Mexica, Zapotec, Mixe and dozens of other Indigenous peoples were not actually swept away by the Spanish conquest nor by the repressive policies of the independent Mexican state. And this is not simply a question of cultural legacy, which is evident in the language, food, traditions and religious syncretism; Indigenous peoples (whom the state insists on categorising as a single group) still live in large areas of the country and take care of their land, defending their communities as best they can. Only by recognising that they, too, have equal status as Mexicans will the Criollo majority perhaps be able to resolve their own dual nature, the schizophrenia of being both European and American, conquerors and conquered, oppressors and victims.

Contents

The photographs in this issue were taken by **Fabio Cuttica**, a documentary photographer born in Rome, who grew up in Colombia and Peru and currently lives in Bogotá. Since 2001 much of his work has focused on Latin America, portraying the region's social, political and cultural dimensions as well as its human rights struggles. He documented the consequences of Colombia's long-running armed conflict in his 'Tierra herida' ('Wounded Earth') project. Between 2010 and 2014 he lived in Mexico, where his images explored phenomena such as migration, conflicts between drug cartels and narcoculture in the city of Tijuana, resulting in his project 'Al borde de la ficción' ('On the Edge of Fiction'), focusing on the world of narco-cinema. In 2016 he joined forces with a group of Colombian and international photographers to set up the OjoRojo Fábrica Visual foundation in Bogotá, an independent space devoted to the promotion, study and popularisation of documentary photography.

Some Numbers

MERCATOR'S LIES

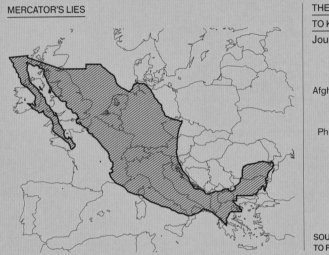

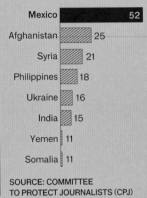
A LOT OF WORK AND NOT MUCH TO SHOW FOR IT

Average hours worked per person employed [→] and GDP per hour worked (US$) [↑], selected OECD countries, 2021

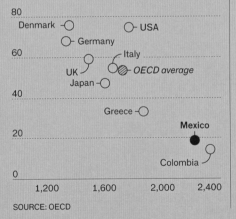

SOURCE: OECD

UNEQUAL ...

Income inequality, selected OECD countries, Gini coefficient (0 = complete equality, 1 = complete inequality), 2021

Pos.		0	1
1	Slovakia		0.222
9	Sweden		0.276
13	France		0.292
15	Germany		0.296
22	Australia		0.318
25	Italy		0.330
31	UK		0.355
33	USA		0.375
36	Mexico		0.420
37	Costa Rica		0.487

SOURCE: OECD

BUBBLES BUBBLES EVERYWHERE

Average annual soft-drink consumption per capita, 2019

🍾 = 25 litres

Chiapas (Mexico)	🍾🍾🍾🍾🍾🍾🍾🍾🍾🍾🍾🍾🍾🍾🍾🍾🍾🍾🍾🍾🍾🍾🍾🍾🍾🍾🍾🍾🍾🍾🍾🍾	821.3
Mexico	🍾🍾🍾🍾🍾🍾	150.0
USA	🍾🍾🍾🍾🍾🍾	146.2
Brazil	🍾🍾🍾	66.2
Japan	🍾🍾	27.4
Russia	🍾🍾	25.6

SOURCE: LATINOMETRICS

THREE OUT OF FOUR

Percentage of population (aged 15+) overweight or obese, selected OECD countries, 2021

Mexico
74.1

USA
73.1

Italy
47.6

Japan
27.2

SOURCE: LATINOMETRICS

Countries with the largest number of native Spanish speakers (millions), 2021

❶
Mexico
124.85

❷
Colombia
50.64

❸
Argentina
44.94

❹
Spain
43.64

❺
USA
41.76

SOURCE: STATISTA

THAT SINKING
FEELING

50 cm/year

The rate at which the historic centre of Mexico City is sinking; Venice, in comparison, sinks 1–2 mm each year

TRAVEL

97.4

million tourists visited Mexico in 2019, almost half (48.3%) of all visits to Central and South America that year

SOURCE: LATINOMETRICS

... MORE EQUAL ...

Women in national government (%), 2000–22

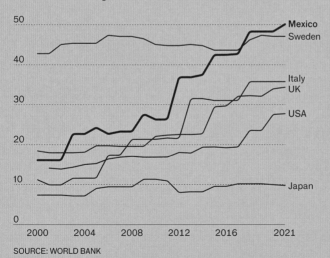

SOURCE: WORLD BANK

... BIODIVERSE

Countries with the greatest biodiversity (Global Biodiversity Index); Mexico is second for reptile species and fourth for mammals

Brazil	512.34
Indonesia	418.78
Colombia	369.76
China	365.84
Mexico	**342.47**
Australia	337.18
Peru	330.12

SOURCE: THE SWIFTEST

The Earth on Loan

JUAN VILLORO
Translated by Kit Maude

Wrapped in a plastic bag for warmth, a migrant
from Honduras travels on the roof of a goods train
to northern Mexico on his way to the US border.

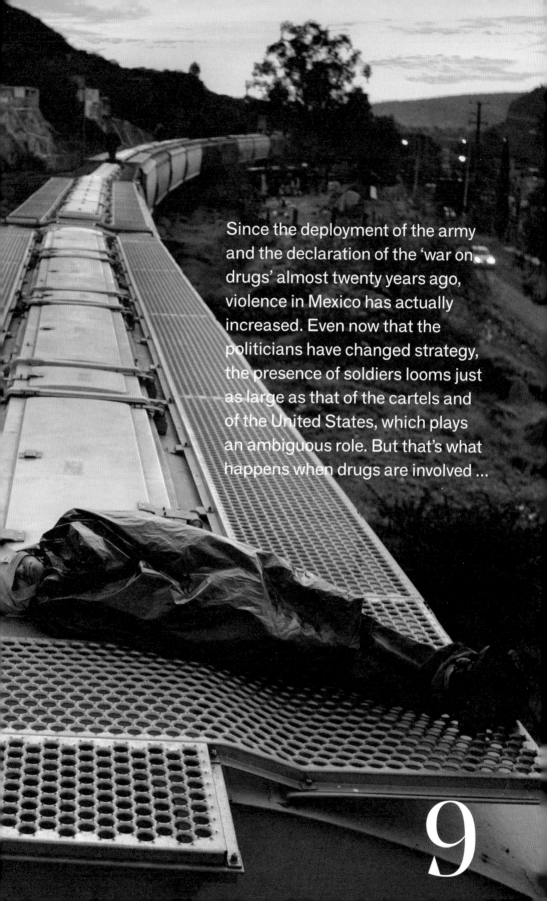

Since the deployment of the army and the declaration of the 'war on drugs' almost twenty years ago, violence in Mexico has actually increased. Even now that the politicians have changed strategy, the presence of soldiers looms just as large as that of the cartels and of the United States, which plays an ambiguous role. But that's what happens when drugs are involved ...

9

Mexico is suffering from its worst outbreak of sustained violence since the Revolution of 1910, and yet the political establishment has turned hiding that truth into a fine art form. In his first governmental report in September 2019, President Andrés Manuel López Obrador dedicated forty seconds to the matter. His approach hasn't shifted in subsequent years, and those who are covering it properly are paying for it with their lives: in 2022 fifteen journalists were murdered.

The Chilean reporter Mónica González has cogently pointed out that the problem of violence in Latin America goes much deeper than drug trafficking; organised crime is a far larger phenomenon, encompassing the cartels but also many more sectors of the economy and government. Today the business elites are more powerful than presidents – even in countries supposedly governed by left-wing administrations such as Chile, Colombia and Mexico – and these elites aren't above indulging in illegality, whether it's putting their money in tax havens or simply laundering it.

In Mexico organised crime controls at least 10 per cent of the money in circulation (a figure that can only be compared with the oil industry or the money sent back from the USA by migrants) and effectively governs sizeable areas that no longer fall under the auspices of the state. In addition to activities that are clearly illegal – such as banditry, kidnapping, human and drug trafficking, fuel smuggling and extorting fees for the use of land – their portfolio includes loans, the export of agricultural goods, mining and clientelist distribution of food, supplies and medicines.

National sovereignty is relative, as was shown by the *El País* journalist Jacobo García in 2019 on his journey through Tierra Caliente in Michoacán, where 70 per cent of the world's avocados are grown (see 'The Cocaine that Washes in from the Sea' on page 29). 'The road of death doesn't run through the Andes or the slopes of Annapurna but along the thirty-six-kilometre stretch of road between Jalisco and Michoacán via Jilotitlán,' he wrote after travelling through areas that reminded him of war zones in Syria, Iraq and Afghanistan.

The country is falling apart and lacks a security policy to address the situation. López Obrador brought an end to the failed policies of predecessors, which favoured an exclusively military approach under great pressure from the USA. The current president arose out of an anti-military, left-wing social movement. He has run for president three times, winning on the third attempt. On each campaign he promised that the army would return to its barracks. However, this isn't so easy to deliver, as the army has become an independent power in its own right. When the Argentinian writer Tomás Eloy Martínez interviewed the former president of

JUAN VILLORO is a Mexican writer, journalist and playwright. A sociologist by training, he is one of the best known intellectuals in Mexico. A number of his works have been translated into English: the novels *The Reef* (2017) and *The Wild Book* (2019), a short-story collection *The Guilty* (2015), as well as *God Is Round: Tackling the Giants, Villains, Triumphs, and Scandals of the World's Favorite Game* (2016) and *Horizontal Vertigo: A City Called Mexico* (2021). He was awarded the prestigious Premio Herralde in 2004 for *El testigo* and won a Rey de España International Journalism Award in 2009 for his investigations into Mexican narco traffickers.

Argentina, Juan Domingo Perón, in exile in Madrid, he asked why, as a soldier, he hadn't called in the army at the crucial moment. The general answered with a maxim: the problem wasn't deploying soldiers on to the streets, it was getting them back into their barracks.

Ever since Felipe Calderón began his 'war on drugs' in 2006, Mexico has been subject to a military occupation that has only increased the violence and other problems suffered by the civilian population. What can be done when troops patrol the streets without providing security? In June 2019, following pressure from Donald Trump, the newly created Mexican National Guard committed itself to detaining Mexican and Central American migrants seeking to reach the USA. Trump threatened to increase taxes on Mexican exports by 5 per cent, which would have been terrible for an economy that, according to the German online data platform Statista, sends 79 per cent of its output to the USA. To avoid an economic shock, the López Obrador administration acceded to the migration demands, and so the Mexican National Guard became an extension of the US Border Patrol.

In 2016, during his presidential campaign, Trump stated that Mexico would pay to build a wall along the border. Once in the White House he found a perverse way of making good his promise: the Mexican Army would become a wall stretching from Central America to the Río Bravo.

Getting back to the issue at hand, the army remains on the streets and is resisting a return to barracks. López Obrador has admitted he had to change his position given the present balance of power. Instead of bringing the army under control, he sought to assign it to other areas, giving it much wider presence

MEXICO'S GREEN GOLD

Fashions and tastes, especially when it comes to food, are unpredictable, sometimes inexplicable. Guacamole is now hugely popular in many parts of the world. It is one of the most commonly consumed accompaniments in Mexico, eaten with many dishes, but especially the fried corn tortilla chips used to make nachos. The ingredients are onion, tomato, lime juice and coriander/cilantro – and, obviously, avocado, the green king of Mexican agriculture, which in 2022 accounted for record exports of 130,000 tonnes to the USA alone. Guacamole has become the star component of the snacks consumed in the USA while watching the Super Bowl and is now an integral part of the American diet, both because of the country's large Mexican population and because of its versatility. In states that produce and export avocados (traditionally Michoacán and more recently Jalisco), avocado cultivation has become an ever more attractive business, leading to disputes over avocado plantations and often violent armed conflicts between entrepreneurial landowners and corrupt politicians, not to mention the paramilitary groups, who are often referred to as 'narcos'. To provide half the world with delicious guacamole, and the revenue generated by a turnover of $500 million, part of the price that Mexico has had to pay is a growing war for the green gold. (F.M.)

in society. The country now finds itself asking itself as to whether the military is becoming more civilian or whether civil society becoming militarised.

It's no bad thing that the National Guard is involved in construction projects, restoring some of the country's artistic heritage, helping victims and patrolling security hot spots, but what are the limits of its power? This question grew more urgent in September 2022 when the Guacamaya collective, which investigates military forces in Latin America, released a report. Of the report's ten terabytes of data, six concern Mexico. Of course, one must handle information that could be plagued with inaccuracies with care, and it's also worth remembering that spies tell lies (something Graham Greene wrote about in his masterful novel *Our Man in Havana*). Even so, there is no doubt that the army is becoming increasingly powerful. Its political sway is clear. A few months ago orders to arrest twelve soldiers linked to the disappearance of forty-three students in Ayotzinapa were rescinded, and the head of the Ministry of Defence, Luis Cresencio Sandoval, refused to appear before Congress to discuss the matter. Later he also refused to meet representatives who came to see him at his office. These acts placed the general above the constitution.

Soon the army is due take charge of customs and an airline as well as hotels on the Yucatán Peninsula. The constitutional reform currently under way will expand the army's presence on the streets until 2029. Does it make sense to empower the troops in this manner when we don't know what kind of government will be in charge in a few years' time?

Again and again the president has betrayed the progressive ideals he claimed to represent and instead acted like a Messianic strongman. His arbitrary exercise of power has not helped the poor he claims to support. In the current state of structural disorder, the three major beneficiaries of this government have been multi-millionaires, organised crime and the army. During his morning tirades, López Obrador accuses anyone who questions his policies of being a conservative, including those further to the left than he is. But there's nothing more conservative than being beholden to the army.

At the dawn of modern German militarism there was a saying: Prussia isn't a country with an army, it's an army with a country. Mexico would appear to be advancing towards its future not with great strides but rather to the beat of a parade-ground drum.

A TOWER OF SKULLS

While the militarisation of Mexico is on the rise, archaeologists are working to exhume vestiges of the Aztec Empire, which offer evidence of violence from long ago. Among these are the notorious *tzompantli*, palisades made out of the skulls of sacrificial victims. Might we see ourselves reflected in these remains if we were to visit the Smoking Mirror of Tezcatlipoca, Lord of Mortality, in which human beings

'Mexico would appear to be advancing towards its future not with great strides but rather to the beat of a parade-ground drum.'

The night of 26–27 September 2014, in Iguala, Guerrero state, three hours south of Mexico City, an armed unit stopped a bus full of students from the Isidro Burgos Rural Teacher Training College in Ayotzinapa. The young people had hijacked a number of buses to travel to the capital to take part in demonstrations planned for 2 October, the anniversary of the 1968 Tlatelolco Massacre. Enrique Peña Nieto's government tried to pin responsibility for the students' disappearance on drug traffickers – a claim that was first made a few hours after the event – and a few months later the then attorney general, Jesús Murillo Karam, who is now in prison, constructed a version of the facts in which the forty-three young *desaparecidos* had been kidnapped by the Guerreros Unidos group, killed and taken to a refuse dump where their bodies were later burned. The official version was contradicted by a group of Argentinian experts in forensic anthropology, who helped to show that the young men were kidnapped with the active participation of the army and police. Since the 1960s forced disappearances have frequently been used as a terror tactic by Mexico's authoritarian governments, but in 2007, with the war on drugs, the number of incidents really began to grow. Official data published in 2022 mentions 111,000 disappearances, but this is only reports submitted. Most cases are not reported out of fear, so the figure could be three or four times higher. Many of the victims were disappeared with the direct or indirect participation of public officials or agents in the security forces. (F.M.)

faced up to their inevitable fate in pre-Hispanic times?

Mexico City has another city lying beneath it. From the ancient Aztec manuscripts and accounts of friars and conquistadors, archaeologists know of the existence of unexplored sites. More than twenty years ago, while I was working on a piece about the capital, experts in urban archaeology told me that they were expecting to find a great deal under Calle de República de Guatemala because it ran along the sacred route of death, which started at the Aztec ballgame courts, where games were played following which either the winner or loser (whoever was best suited for sacrifice) was offered up to the gods. However, excavation was hindered by the fact that these treasures lay beneath colonial-era buildings that cannot be demolished.

Occasionally an earthquake might give archaeologists a helping hand. Calle Guatemala has revealed its secrets thanks to collapses and cracks that opened up during the last two such events. In 2015 an extremely important relic of ancient Mexico's peculiar relationship with death was discovered: an immense *tzompantli*. At 24 Calle Guatemala the base of a tower of skulls dedicated to Huitzilopochtli, the God of the Sun and of War, was unearthed. During the conquest Andrés Tapia, one of Hernán Cortés's soldiers, reckoned he'd counted 136,000 skulls, while Friar Diego Durán made it 80,000, both figures almost certainly exaggerated by the reverential fear inspired by the morbid monument. In his book *Muerte a filo de obsidiana* ('Death by Obsidian Blade'), the archaeologist Eduardo Matos Moctezuma, who started excavating the Grand Temple in 1978, describes the *tzompantli* as 'the clearest manifestation of the political and religious control' that the hierarchy of priests and soldiers exercised over their people.

In October 2016 archaeologist Raúl Barrera took charge of the work at 24 Calle Guatemala. The site had not yet been opened to the public, but I was able to visit on 16 November 2017, two months after the earthquake that had flattened several buildings in the city. Wooden crossbeams supported the walls. A few metres further on, the Museo del Templo Mayor had a stone model of a *tzompantli* on display. Because it was just a representation, the incredible geometry of death remained abstract. In contrast, the collection of skulls that slowly emerged from the soil at number 24 had an unnerving authenticity with its thousands of hollow eye sockets that had been staring at nothing for the past five hundred years.

According to Barrera, most of those sacrificed were prisoners of war, but there are also some Spanish skulls. The most important revelation has been that 20 per cent of the skulls belonged to women and 10 per cent to children. In the sacrificial economy of the Aztecs, whose goal was to appease capricious gods, one had to make offerings of prisoners but also give up one's nearest and dearest. It would be completely wrong to think that the ancient Mexicans behaved this way out of a disdain for life; on the contrary, it was extremely precious to them, the only thing able to pacify the anger of the gods. The sacrifices would only be effective if the suffering was shared.

The tower of skulls, almost five metres in diameter, enhanced the political and religious power of Tenochtitlan. It was a stage surrounded by a city of 250,000 inhabitants.

Confronted with this incredible relationship with death, it is important to remember what Georges Dumézil wrote about the 'oddities' of the past: interpreting 'archaic religious events' in proper context means putting to one side the 'misleading barbarities one learns about in school'. In *La muerte entre los mexicas* ('Death Among the Mexica'), Matos Moctezuma interprets the *tzompantli* thus: 'The gods, sometimes belligerent, sometimes benevolent, had to receive sacrifices of different kinds in order to play their roles within the structure of the universe. One of man's most valued possessions is one's life, so the sacrifice of that life ensures to a great degree the continuation of the processes that make life possible.'

Sacrifice was a prayer; you fed the sun so it would keep rising.

At 24 Calle Guatemala the soil is still damp from the lagoon that was covered over to build Mexico City. Here the air has grown thicker with time, and the skulls make the present even more eerie. The world of Aztec sacrifice, which we find so strange, makes us shiver. The most surprising aspect of it, however, is that it can be decoded.

The same cannot be said of our time. In comparison with their cosmology, contemporary Mexico seems even more absurd. How can we explain a country of secret graves (more than two thousand of which have been uncovered in the past fourteen years), where death is little more than a by-product of plunder?

150 SHOTS IN THREE MINUTES

At 6.35 a.m. on 26 June 2020 a van blocked Paseo de la Reforma, the venerable avenue in Mexico City, and twenty-eight assassins opened fire on the car of Omar García Harfuch, the secretary of citizens' security. The head of the Mexico City police was travelling with two bodyguards, who were killed in the fusillade, as was a passing street vendor. García Harfuch survived thanks to the vehicle's Level-5 armour. Three hours after the attack he

A young woman outside a house riddled with bullet holes in Culiacán, Sinaloa state.

wrote on Twitter: 'This morning we were victims of a cowardly attack by the CJNG [Jalisco New Generation Cartel] ... I was hit by three bullets and several pieces of shrapnel.'

The attackers were repelled by four bodyguards travelling in another car, which was out of the line of fire, and by police who arrived a minute later. Twenty-one suspects were arrested of whom fourteen were charged. The attack was a notable failure. However, what stuck in the mind wasn't the incompetence of those who let off more than 150 bullets, most of which missed their primary target, but the spectacular nature of the operation, its daring theatricality. The priority wasn't to kill but to show that this could be possible right in the heart of the Mexican capital.

Drug traffickers have been visibly flexing their power while the government steps back. López Obrador began his administration with appeals to the morality of the kingpins. He asked them to think 'of their families, their mothers, their *mamacitas*', urging them to dispense 'hugs not bullets', and used an infantile expression of disgust, '¡*Fuchi, caca!*' ('Ugh, poop!'). Meanwhile, the murders increased. The BBC reported that in 2019 34,582 criminal homicides were committed, 2.5 per cent more than in 2018, up until then the bloodiest year in recent Mexican history.

THE ARMED PEACE

Admirably, López Obrador called for an end to the policies of the war on drugs that the conservative president, Felipe Calderón, had borrowed from the Nixon administration and Plan Colombia. The

'Fighting fire with fire could only ever result in one thing: every Mexican becoming potential collateral damage.'

policy was inaugurated by Calderón in December 2006, two weeks after he took office, while the opposition was still questioning the election results. He explained his decision thus: two weeks after taking power he 'encountered' a problem he hadn't foreseen and so turned to the army.

The real causes would appear to have been quite different. The Partido Acción Nacional (National Action Party, PAN) politician was perfectly aware of the country's security problems, but he couldn't make promises that he would use the armed forces while on the campaign trail. Once he became president he didn't send a bill to be considered by Congress or discuss the matter with his party. The war on drugs was a personal initiative designed to change the public conversation. While tens of thousands were calling for a revision of the electoral proceedings, the tanks took to the streets, and suddenly that was all anyone could talk about.

There was no consensus regarding the mobilisation of the army, and it was premature. Calderón was facing an enemy of unknown strength, whose tentacles already reached into the government itself, with no conception of where the front lines or rearguard might be. Six years later a hundred thousand had been confirmed dead and thirty thousand more had disappeared, the kind of figures one sees in a civil war. Consequently PAN came third in the next elections.

Throughout his administration Calderón insisted that the increase in violence was caused by territorial wars between the cartels, describing the narcos as 'evildoers', strangers who had latched on to the community, unable to see that they were a part of the social fabric. The discourse of the government – which was, by and large, the tack followed by the media – constructed a fiction in which the criminals formed part of an anti-society committed to annihilating itself, while inadvertently causing collateral damage to the civilian population. The solution to this multifaceted problem with its different social factors and diplomatic, cultural, political, religious and public-health-related nuances, could never be solely military. Fighting fire with fire could only ever result in one thing: every Mexican becoming potential collateral damage.

Frustration over the bloodshed meant that in the 2012 elections the country decided to bring back the Partido Revolucionaria Institucional (Institutional Revolutionary Party, PRI), the antiquated organisation that had been in power from 1929 to 2000, whose only nod towards modernisation was the fact that its candidate, Enrique Peña Nieto, looked better on TV than he did in the flesh. Near my home a line of graffiti explained rather succinctly why the antiheroes of Mexican politics were back: 'Out with the incompetent and in with the corrupt'.

From 2012 onwards the official line

shifted. Where Calderón put the military at the centre of his government and posed for photographs wearing a uniform that was – much like the level of responsibility required to govern the country – far too big for him, Peña Nieto believed that the violence was a problem of perception, one that could be resolved if it simply wasn't mentioned. In this spirit of evasion he called for a 'turning of the page' regarding the Ayotzinapa case, hoping to make those who had disappeared in real life disappear from our memories as well.

López Obrador doesn't belong to the kleptocracy that governed the country for almost a century for its own gain, and neither is he willing to implement the repressive policies of the PRI or the PAN. His government, backed by thirty million votes, appears to be a reset when compared with previous ways of doing politics. However, that's not enough for success. His alliance with evangelists and the most powerful businesspeople in the country, disdain for the middle classes, support for fossil fuels, determinedly strongman style and ill-advised treatment of environmentalists, feminists, scientists, Indigenous peoples and the victims of violence amount to the actions of a conservative populist who occasionally ventures into left-wing territory. His attacks on various sectors have seen his support eroded, but his social base is still broad, and this has allowed him to wield power in an authoritarian manner with little time for teamwork or the involvement of experts.

Populism thrives on polarisation. In 2016 Russia didn't campaign openly on Trump's behalf; its tactics were more subtle. Russian programmers established spaces of polarisation on the internet, creating and supporting contradictory causes to stimulate confrontation. As the digital sphere grew more fraught, the person offering the most extreme solutions received greater support. López Obrador has been acting in a similar manner from his position as President of the Republic. At his morning conferences he calls out his supposed foes and dissenting journalists by name. He has transformed critical judgement into betrayal of the motherland, ignoring the fact that some challenges can actually improve policies and strengthen the government. In an environment where journalists are routinely murdered, the Mexican president is questioning every truth he doesn't agree with.

SOPHOCLES IN SINALOA
Joaquín 'El Chapo' Guzmán is the most infamous drug trafficker in Mexico. This reputation has had a range of repercussions across different sectors of society. As a notorious villain who has now been arrested, the blame for everything can fall exclusively on him. Guzmán isn't well educated, doesn't speak English and isn't very good with technology, but the media and government assure us that he runs businesses in more than fifty countries. It has been proved that he has committed many atrocities, but it is possible that others have been attributed to him to take the heat off criminals who remain at large. So the government benefits from having arrested the man 'guilty of everything', and El Chapo's rivals and partners accuse him of crimes that continue to be committed.

In July 2019 Joaquín Guzmán received a sentence of a severity that matches his crimes (life in prison plus thirty years), which he is currently serving in the most secure prison in the USA, the ADX Supermax in Colorado. Putting a 'king of evil', a Wizard of Oz who ruled an entire kingdom, behind bars has become a

MYTHOLOGISING THE NARCOS

In recent years, when talk turns to Mexico, you might well think about TV series such as *Narcos*. Cocaine trafficking, snakeskin boots, AK-47s, menacing glares and shootouts have become part of the country's image in the global collective imagination. And the most famous of all Mexican drug traffickers is Joaquín Guzmán Loera, aka 'El Chapo' ('Shorty'), head of the Sinaloa Cartel and currently residing in a US jail. A deeper reading of Mexico's history, on the other hand, shows the drug trafficking groups playing a subordinate role to an authoritarian state with comprehensive control of the country. As the academic Oswaldo Zavala (author of *Drug Cartels Do Not Exist: Narcotrafficking in US and Mexican Culture*) has explained, the drug traffickers have always been subordinate and have had to pay handsomely for permission to move drugs and control territory. The most feared bosses with the highest profile in the media are portrayed as princes of evil, whereas, in fact, they are replaceable and rather pathetic when they leave the stage. This is true of El Chapo, who was painted as a diabolical, almost omnipotent, figure but fell into the police's net in 2016 because he wanted to meet the *telenovela* star Kate del Castillo and pitch a TV series about his life. Between 1990 and 2006 Mexico saw a drop in violent crime. Former president Felipe Calderón's war on drugs was justified as being a response to the violence – although Calderón himself has since faced accusations of links with drug trafficking – but it was actually the militarisation of the country, also pursued by Calderón's successor Enrique Peña Nieto, that led to the increase in murders and disappearances among civilians, keeping the criminal groups subordinate to the state. (F.M.)

Opposite: President Andrés Manuel López Obrador addresses a rally. **Above**: A man prays to the Virgin of Guadalupe at a migrant shelter in Ixtepec, southern Mexico.

convenient pretext for ending the search for other guilty parties.

There's not much point in getting rid of the leader of a criminal gang if it just keeps operating under another leader. This is a structural issue that can't be solved simply by arresting an iconic figure, but every now and again, for publicity reasons and for political interests, a kingpin is arbitrarily picked up.

Shortly after El Chapo was sentenced, at lunchtime on 17 October 2019 his son Ovidio was arrested by anti-narcotics police in Culiacán. The Sinaloa Cartel reacted with a backlash that saw sixty-eight military vehicles riddled with bullet holes, eight people killed, sixteen wounded, nineteen roadblocks and a prison mutiny during which forty-five inmates escaped. It was 32 degrees Celsius in the capital of Sinaloa that day, but the fires made it even hotter. In this incendiary climate, a narco negotiating the release of 'El Chapito' addressed the military with haughty superiority. 'We are talking to you politely. Let him go and leave, and no one's going to do anything to you. Otherwise you'll get it up the ass.'

Under such pressure López Obrador ordered the release of Ovidio Guzmán. 'Capturing one criminal can't be worth more than people's lives,' he explained. The statement contrasts with that of Calderón to justify *his* strategy: 'It will cost innocent lives, but it's still worth

'In this incendiary climate, a narco negotiating the release of "El Chapito" addressed the military with haughty superiority. "We are talking to you politely. Let him go and leave, and no one's going to do anything to you. Otherwise you'll get it up the ass."'

going ahead.' The failed arrest was dubbed Black Thursday, or the Culiacanazo, the Battle of Culiacán.

Although it was the lesser evil, there was no consensus about the news in the fragmented country. López Obrador appealed to the humanitarian side of justice, but to many it suggested weakness. The magazine *Proceso* ran a front page with the headline: 'You're in Charge'.

It's a more complex issue than it might seem. In his excellent article 'The Temptation of War', Oswaldo Zavala, a professor at City University of New York and author of the book *Drug Cartels Do Not Exist: Narcotrafficking in US and Mexican Culture* (Vanderbilt University Press, 2021), noted that the Culiacán operation was ordered by the Drug Trafficking Information Analysis Group, possibly in coordination with the DEA and the Sinaloa government, which was then run by the PRI, in accordance with the parameters of American intervention agreed by Calderón under the 2008 Mérida Initiative. A month before the capture, on 16 September, Uttam Dhillon, at the time interim director of the DEA, was in Culiacán. Zavala doesn't rule out the many flaws in the operation having been intentional and designed to discredit the government. Questions about the failed capture led some to wonder in whose interest it is to revive the war on drugs.

'The military occupation and paramilitarisation of Mexico have been a means of clearing and illegally appropriating land to make way for megaprojects involving the extraction of natural resources such as gas, oil and mining,' answers Zavala in a piece in the *Post Opinión* (5 November 2019).

Two and a half thousand years ago, in *Antigone*, Sophocles contrasted the rights of the individual with one's obligations to the state. López Obrador prevented a massacre and set free a powerful enemy. Public opinion, the modern version of the Greek chorus, decided that this looked like surrender, similar to the reaction, in January 2020, to the president shaking the hand of El Chapo's mother while refusing to meet the victims of violence led by the poet Javier Sicilia. The president was chided by the chorus, but 'Athens' backed him: his approval rating in October 2022 was 69 per cent, according to the research company Morning Consult. In the 2021 elections his party won the governorship of Sinaloa for the first time, showing that the political hopes awoken by Moreno, the president's party, trumped the fallout from of the Battle of Culiacán.

Ovidio's arrest remained unfinished business until 5 January 2023, when Culiacán suffered another Black Thursday. El Chapo's son was arrested again early that morning on the outskirts of the city. The

THE PASSENGER Juan Villoro

previous operation had failed because it had been carried out in the city centre. But, even so, the narco's bodyguards made their presence felt in this unofficial civil war: ten soldiers and nineteen criminals were killed, about twenty blockades were set up around the city and the army's armoured vehicles came under fire from fifty-calibre artillery. The bullets even strafed an Aeroméxico commercial flight, causing panic among the passengers.

The battle took place on the eve of President Joe Biden's visit to Mexico, making Black Thursday a kind of gift for Twelfth Night.

THE USA'S BACKYARD:
THE DEA UNDERCOVER

Every day two thousand weapons enter Mexico illegally, while two hundred are decommissioned. The figures are, of course, approximate, but they reflect the difficulty of monitoring the busiest border in the world. It's not easy to combat drug trafficking when you live next door to the largest consumer of drugs on the planet. 'You supply the nostrils, we supply the bodies,' as the Uruguayan author Eduardo Galeano once wrote.

The tense relationship between Mexico and the USA came to a dramatic head when, in October 2020, police in Los Angeles arrested General Salvador Cienfuegos, who had been secretary of defence in the government of Enrique Peña Nieto. Such a high-profile Mexican official had never been arrested before, and it caused great controversy. Certain sectors entertained the hope that another country might step in to establish an order of which Mexico is incapable, but it also raised issues about sovereignty and international cooperation.

On 8 December 2022 Tim Golden, an experienced journalist and Pulitzer Prize winner, published a long report in *The New York Times* on the investigation that led to the capture and subsequent release of General Cienfuegos, 'The Cienfuegos Affair: Inside the Case that Upended the Drug War in Mexico'. The text is revealing for how detailed its information is and for the unusual way in which the United States treats its 'backyard' – that is, Mexico. Golden shadows members of the DEA, judges and prosecutors fighting the war on drugs. He implicitly makes the assumption that, in contrast to Mexican officials, the intentions of the agents from *his* country are honourable, which seems doubtful in an environment so awash with blood and money. Golden offers an in-depth account of the work of the DEA on Mexican soil but never seems to feel the need to clarify that *this is a clandestine operation in a foreign country.*

When Calderón signed the Mérida Initiative in 2007, for which, over the course of fifteen years, the Mexican government received $3.5 billion in military aid from the USA, he agreed to adopt the USA's strategy but never achieved the tactical successes that the Colombian president, Álvaro Uribe, had enjoyed with Plan Colombia.

López Obrador cancelled the Mérida Initiative, altered the navy's relationship with its advisors from the USA, ordered the closure of the Sensitive Investigation Units – where Mexican agents operated under DEA supervision – and rejected a range of plans for cooperation with the US embassy. According to Golden, this resulted in Matthew Donahue, the head of the DEA in Mexico, starting to act independently of the Mexican government with the support (reluctant initially, subsequently more enthusiastic) of Christopher Landau, who was US ambassador between 2019 and 2021. The DEA thus

Top: Members of the community police in Guerrero state march through the streets of San Luis de Acatlán.
Bottom: A musician plays in a cemetery in Ciudad Juárez on the Day of the Dead, when the dead are remembered with festivities and music.

President Andrés Manuel López Obrador (AMLO) had promised a new security strategy based on 'hugs not bullets', in other words investing in social programmes that would take away manpower from criminal activities and disbanding the corrupt Federal Police to incorporate it into an 'incorruptible' National Guard. The transition was not painless, however. Many former police officers refused because it would have meant pay cuts, while others complained of not being treated as the soldiers' equals; above all, serious strategic deficiencies have emerged. Intelligence capabilities in the fight against organised crime seem significantly diminished, and there has been no shortage of shadowy goings-on and interference in security policy. The infamous operation to arrest El Chapo's son in 2019 was not approved either by the president or his security cabinet, leaving doubts over who is actually in charge, and it constituted the most significant crisis in the policy of pacification. The feeling is that the power of the cartels has increased, as has the violence. In spite of the hugs there are more bullets. AMLO boasts that the murder rate fell by 3 per cent in the first three years of his presidency, but at the same time there have been five times as many displaced people fleeing violence. The transfer of civilian duties to the military, the other plank of AMLO's strategy, has also led to problems. In some cases these new activities, such as the Tren Maya project and the running of some airports (there is also talk of an airline), mean that the military will be able to raise funds independently, leading to a risk of it becoming even more of a state within a state.

wreaked political vengeance and acted with impunity on foreign soil, justifying its behaviour with an argument – hard to refute – that the Mexican government was incapable of investigating itself.

Donahue identified thirty-five officials as being potentially involved with the narcos, homing in on the PRI governor of Nayarit, Roberto Sandoval Castañeda, and his attorney-general, Edgar Veytia, who cooperated with the 'H' gang, which acted under the protection of a high-ranking military commander known as 'Zepeda', the maternal surname of Cienfuegos. He managed to get a judge in Brooklyn interested in the case.

His 'evidence' was based on intercepted messages from the phones of two H members. One of them described the 'godfather' as 'Salbador Sinfuego Sepeda'. Another source was Veytia himself, following his arrest. However, the former public attorney only repeated what the H members had said, offering one flimsy piece of additional information. In a safe house he learned that one of the H operatives was being tortured on the floor below and heard him shout, 'I'm one of Cienfuegos's men!' Was this an infiltrator working to break up the cartel, which is what happened shortly afterwards? Was he a desperate narco looking for a way out by appealing to the head of the armed forces? Whatever the truth, an anguished cry hardly counts as evidence.

Cienfuegos allegedly took bribes from the Nayarita Cartel. His way of life hadn't changed, and he hadn't moved or purchased any more properties. When Landau asked about this, the agents turned their conjecture into an accusation – 'A fortune like that is easy to hide in Mexico.'

Shortly afterwards, the navy decimated the H gang, and so the case against Cienfuegos was built on the intercepted

'If one is to combat violence, then one cannot use it unnecessarily. The ethical strength of this position is clear, but it's not enough to pacify a country.'

messages of two dead criminals. Not exactly solid grounds.

Donahue knew that López Obrador didn't allow extraditions so took advantage of the general being on holiday with his family in the USA and arrested him at Los Angeles Airport in October 2020. The Mexican secretary of foreign affairs, Marcelo Ebrard, immediately spoke to the US attorney-general William Barr – who claimed to know nothing of the affair – as well as the US ambassador. 'I'd never seen Marcelo so upset,' noted Landau. Ebrard accused them of operating in secret and showing a lack of respect for Mexico. 'Would you treat France this way?' he demanded.

The DEA had prepared a 700-plus-page brief full of inconsistencies that the Mexican government published after the general had been freed, to the humiliation of the agency, which was hoping to find decisive evidence *a posteriori* during the pre-trial interrogations.

Tim Golden's long article suggests, rightly, that there are too many loose ends in the fight against drugs – but it also describes a hurried investigation, the motives of which could easily range from a genuine search for the truth to the desire of agents and public attorneys to further their careers with a high-profile bust.

The meaning of texts can change depending on who is reading them. 'The Cienfuegos Affair' means something different to those of us who regard Mexico as a country rather than someone's backyard. Golden provides compelling evidence of the USA's invasive strategy and the firm stand taken, in this instance, by President López Obrador and Secretary of Foreign Affairs Ebrard against excessive foreign intervention.

None of this lifts suspicion about the complicity of high-ranking military figures with drug trafficking – organised crime depends on it – however, the dominant narrative generally pins all the blame on Mexico. Even though every police station in the United States has an internal affairs section, we know very little about the police's ties with crime there. But if such ties didn't exist we surely wouldn't be describing the country as the biggest consumer of narcotics in the world. With admirable efficiency the DEA, the CIA, the FBI and other agencies have managed to institutionalise the drug trade while focusing on avoiding its more violent repercussions. At the same time they have created a narrative that identifies the origins of the problem as being located in Mexico, Colombia and other countries. And so the corruption of American officials is shrouded in silence. Even an article as wide ranging and well researched as Tim Golden's follows the moral compass established by that narrative: the stories are to be found in the south; the ones up north can't be told.

THE MESSAGE OF THE BONES

In 2010 Felipe Calderón ordered that the bones of the Heroes of Independence be exhumed so they could be taken on a tour the country in a grand funeral procession. The remains of the founding fathers formed a mobile *tzompantli* that suited the hypervisibility of power sought by the PAN president in his war on drugs.

To his credit, in his campaign rhetoric López Obrador rejected this approach, but he hasn't been able to keep his promises. Today the army is larger and the strategy weaker. According to *The New York Times*, in 2021 the Mexican National Guard, which is three times the size of the now-defunct Federal Police, arrested 8,258 criminals, only 38 per cent of the number of arrests made in 2018 before the unified force was created.

Politics begins with words, but it must move on from them. In 1867 Victor Hugo sent a letter to Mexican president Benito Juárez, calling on him to spare the life of the ousted Mexican Emperor Maximilian: 'Let the violator of principles be saved by a principle. Let him have that joy and shame.' The biggest snub one can give an adversary is to not act like them. If one is to combat violence, then one cannot use it unnecessarily. The ethical strength of this position is clear, but it is not enough to pacify a country. In his rhetorical outbursts López Obrador has not offered any concrete plans for restoring the social fabric. To a wide array of questions he answers that he will act 'honestly', a principle very rarely observed by his predecessors, but it won't guarantee him control of the playing field.

The pre-Hispanic world paid religious homage to death. For warriors, to fall in battle was an honour and a sacrifice to demanding gods. However, at the same time Aztec poets lamented this vassalage in verses full of anguish and sadness at the fleeting nature of things. Like a samurai composing a haiku before committing hara-kiri, the Aztec poet both laments and accepts his inevitable fate. Dying is painful, which is why the gods value the gesture.

How can we compare these practices with the gratuitousness of death in contemporary Mexico? In 2021, as archaeologists were unearthing the skulls of the *tzompantli*, the five-hundredth anniversary of the fall of Tenochtitlan was marked. Images of these ceremonial skull racks cause shivers to run down your spine but, as noted, they had a clear religious motive. In contrast, the bones of the forefathers put on show by Felipe Calderón weren't much more than a circus sideshow.

Today Mexico is one big necropolis, seeded everywhere with contemporary skulls. We live, as the journalist Marcela Turati, who has investigated the issue in depth, puts it, in 'the country of two thousand mass graves'.

Every relic has a reason to be. Is there meaning in any of this spilled blood?

In the bloodiest era of our history the voice of a Náhuatl poet rings out: 'On the earth that was loaned to us, nothing is so uncertain as life.' 🖋

Mexico's Last Four Presidents

FEDERICO MASTROGIOVANNI

Vicente Fox Quesada

2000–6

Born in Mexico City in 1942, he grew up in the conservative, Catholic state of Guanajuato and was the first Mexican president to represent the right-wing Catholic National Action Party (PAN). A businessman in the farming sector, in the 1970s he was president of the Mexican division of Coca-Cola. His government was the first to interrupt the seventy-year reign of the Institutional Revolutionary Party (PRI) which led to expectations being very high. He is remembered for his efforts to reach agreements on migration policy with the USA, for his opposition to the Iraq War and for having removed Fidel Castro from a dinner in 2002 to make way for George W. Bush with the famous phrase 'You eat and go.' Today he is one of the main advocates for the legalisation of drugs in Mexico.

Felipe Calderón Hinojosa

2006–12

Born in Morelia, Michoacán, in 1962, his conservative, right-wing PAN government began with a large-scale militarisation of the country in his war on drugs; a memorable image is of him dressed in military fatigues at the beginning of his term. In reality the strategy led to the deaths of more than 100,000 people during his tenure and a 200 per cent increase in homicide rates compared with the previous period. He is also remembered for Operation Fast and Furious, under which 2,500 weapons were illegally imported from the USA between 2009 and 2011, ending up in the hands of various criminal groups. His secretary of public security, the extremely powerful and greatly feared Genaro García Luna, was found guilty by a Brooklyn court in February 2023 of having taken millions of dollars in bribes from the cartels he should have been fighting. Calderón currently lives in Spain.

Enrique Peña Nieto

2012–18

He was born in Atlacomulco, state of Mexico, in 1966 in one of the strongholds of the PRI, the party he remained faithful to throughout his political career and which, under various names, governed Mexico without interruption from 1929 to 2000. In early 2014 he received the backing of *Time* magazine, which put him on its front cover under the headline 'Saving Mexico'. His time in office is remembered for the privatisation of Mexico's energy resources in his 2013 reform, the 'White House' scandal in which a mansion worth $7 million was given to the first lady by the government's leading contractor and the disappearance of forty-three students from the teacher training college in Ayotzinapa in September 2014, one of the most tragic events in Mexico's recent history, in which elements of the army and the security forces were involved. To this day the young men remain among the ranks of the *desaparecidos*.

Andrés Manuel López Obrador (AMLO)

2018–24

Born in 1953 in Macuspana in the sweltering state of Tabasco in south-eastern Mexico, AMLO is known as 'Pejelagarto' after a freshwater fish typical of the region. In 2006 and 2012 he made unsuccessful bids to become president with a left-wing party, having previously served as governor of Tabasco state and Mexico City, and only in 2018 did he achieve his objective with a landslide victory for Morena, the National Regeneration Movement. Considered a populist by his opponents, he takes inspiration from Benito Juárez and Lázaro Cárdenas, and since the beginning of his mandate he has described his government as the 'fourth transformation', following Mexico's three other transformations: independence, Benito Juárez's reforms and the Revolution of 1910. His government's main priorities are the fight against corruption, economic support for the poorest in society under the slogan '*primero los pobres*', pacifying the country after years of what Felipe Calderón called the 'war on drugs', nationalisation of energy and environmental resources and the modernisation of infrastructure.

In a remote village on the Caribbean coast on the border with Belize, the locals have turned to *playear*, beachcombing for packages of drugs driven onshore by the wind.

JACOBO GARCÍA
Translated by Sonia Verjovsky

The crystal-clear waters of the Caribbean, in the state of Quintana Roo, one of the most popular holiday destinations anywhere in Mexico.

The Cocaine that Washes in from the Sea

The last man in Mexico lives at 18°12′9″N and 87°50′36″W. This is where you'll find him, more often than not on the roof of his house. Don Luis's home faces the Caribbean, and surrounding it, wherever you look, is mangrove swamp. If he walks five minutes to his right, he's in a different country, but if he walks for an hour to his left he reaches Xcalak, the first village in Mexico.

Don Luis is a sinewy 58-year-old with dark hair and a moustache who lives in an abandoned house on one of the most absurd borders in the world – a line and a military base that splits a ninety-nine-kilometre cay in two, leaving a piece of land in the south-east of Mexico that runs parallel to the coast of Belize. The northern section, which belongs to Mexico, is an unpopulated area sixty-two kilometres in length, while the southern part, which is in Belize, is thirty-seven kilometres long, and it would be impossible to squeeze even one more tourist into it.

The last man in Mexico has no electricity, running water or land access to his house. He has no fridge, television or fan, and occasionally his old phone picks up the signal from Belize. But he knows things that may seem impossible to other mere mortals, such as how to fish with a shoelace, how to desalinate seawater, how to plant seeds on the beach or how to suck out the venom if bitten by a *nauyaca*, one of the deadliest pit vipers anywhere in the world.

Luis Méndez was born in Mérida, Yucatán, and was a civil servant until an acquaintance suggested he become a warden at the estate. Three years after reaching this furthest-flung corner of Mexico he has learned that everything that comes from the sea has some use: a piece of string to jump-start a propeller, the sole of a shoe fashioned into a hinge, a bottle top to secure a nail.

Every day, as soon as the sun comes up, Don Luis goes out for a walk in the company of his dog Canelo, a brown Hungarian Vizsla. He used to walk along the sand, but now they traipse over a foul-smelling carpet of sargassum, the gulf-weed that invades the Caribbean and gives off an unbearable stench of rotten egg along the shore.

On the day I go with him, along the

JACOBO GARCÍA is a Spanish journalist who has been a correspondent in Latin America for more than twenty years, first for *El Mundo*, then for the Associated Press news agency and since 2017 for *El País* in Mexico and Central America. He has covered more than thirty elections on the continent, two coups and many natural disasters, including the earthquake in Haiti. He has also worked in the Middle East and, more recently, in Ukraine. He has collaborated with *Clarín* (Argentina), *Soho* (Colombia), *El Universal* (Mexico), CNN and *La Tercera* (Chile).

'During our walk I hear a new verb for the first time, *playear*, to beachcomb, to carry out the dogged search for cocaine bricks dropped along the shore from small planes. If you don't beachcomb here, you're really not playing the game.'

brown mass strewn with tin cans, flip-flops, bleach bottles, lids and potato-chip containers, there are also hundreds of plastic bags the size of the palm of a hand. They're all the same, half open and with a residue of white powder and seawater.

Don Luis wakes up every morning right across from the world's second largest coral reef, but he walks with his eyes glued to the ground. He says he is simply going out to make sure everything is in order, but during our walk I hear a new verb for the first time, *playear*, to beachcomb, to carry out the dogged search for cocaine bricks dropped along the shore from small planes. If you don't beachcomb here, you're really not playing the game.

This Robinson of the Caribbean is an affable man who only slips on his shoes to walk down the beach. He can recognise every kind of engine that passes by his house simply from its hum, and he goes on to demonstrate.

'A light aircraft goes grooooooongggg,' he illustrates in a long-drawn-out way, 'but a fifteen-horsepower boat goes brrr-rrrrrrrr, pause, brrrrrrrrrrr, and then another pause to remove the gulfweed from the propeller,' he explains. 'The forty-horsepower one goes nyeeeeeeeeee,' he says, moving his closed fist in the air from side to side as if it were the accelerator. 'And the seventy-five ...' He makes a noise just like the previous one but deeper and with an 'o'. And he continues until he reaches the hundred-horsepower engine,

at which point he deploys a wide-ranging, guttural orchestra of sounds.

Don Luis can also identify the whistles he hears rising from the sea at night – the ones indicating 'they're coming', 'hurry up' or 'let's go' – and whether it's El Gavilancito (the Sparrow), La Zorra (the Fox), El Pelón (Baldy), El Guanaco (the Salvadoran) who is doing the whistling ...

The last man in Mexico may not have Netflix, but all he has to do is sit on his balcony to be able to watch the high-speed boat races, police chases and planes flying furtively over. He recalls the scene from the day before, when he sat down with his wife Norma to enjoy the evening show, and says, 'There were so many mosquitos that I had to burn some coconuts so we wouldn't have to move back inside.'

*

The Caribbean contains 1,061 islands belonging to thirty-two nations – a region and culture of its own that Colombian writer Gabriel García Márquez described as the only country that is made not of land but water.

Waxing less lyrical, for Mexicans the Caribbean refers to the 1,176 kilometres of coast that stretches between Don Luis's house and Cape Catoche at the tip of the Yucatán Peninsula. This includes areas such as Cancún, Playa del Carmen, Cozumel and the Riviera Maya – in other words, 35 per cent of the tourist revenue of the sixth most visited country in the →

Jacobo García'a article 'The Cocaine that Washes in from the Sea' – winner of the True Story Award 2020-1 and the Premio Gabo 2020 – forms part of an ambitious editorial project (a collaboration between the Spanish newspaper *El País* and *El Faro*, the first online newspaper in Latin America, founded in 1998 in El Salvador) to publish six long-form essays covering the southern border of Mexico. The piece reprinted here is section one (of three) of the first chapter, 'The Murky Waters of the Caribbean', set on the Mexican side of the three-way border with Belize and Guatemala. It is available in Spanish and English on the *País* website, along with maps, videos and interviews: elpais.com/especiales/2019/frontera-sur. The project was curated by José Luis Sanz (director of *El Faro*) and the deputy-director of *El País América* Javier Lafuente. Here they discuss their motivation for undertaking the project.

The Forgotten Border of the Americas

JOSÉ LUIS SANZ AND JAVIER LAFUENTE
Translated by Kit Maude

It has been ignored for decades. The strip of land that connects Mexico to Central America doesn't have the photogenic impact of a wall or the mystique lent by American films and media to the Río Bravo or the Arizona desert. Instead, it has been seen as just another Latin American border: chaotic, wild, porous and silent. However, every day it's the most widely traversed frontier on the American continent and one of the busiest in the world, obligatory passage for the hundreds of thousands of Central Americans headed north on foot. More than 120,000 migrants crossing this border were detained annually in Mexico in recent years. It is estimated that about 90 per cent of the cocaine that reaches the United States will have spent some time on Central American soil before slipping across the border with Mexico. In short, it makes no sense to discuss migration, drug trafficking or any other issue related to the region without taking this border into account as well.

And yet knowledge about this frontier 5,000 kilometres away from its northern counterpart is sketchy. Its remoteness from the United States accentuates the

remote corners of this frontier. Other communities, such as the Mennonites of Belize, have found these forgotten lands to be the perfect place in which to settle and build a life for themselves. In many areas the state is a vague concept. Almost all the security policies of successive Mexican governments over the past three decades have used this strip of land, in which North America thins into an isthmus, as a base, but neither the implementation nor the failure of said policies has earned much more than a passing mention elsewhere. Thus far, the southern border has lived and evolved far from prying eyes and awkward questions.

Donald Trump's anti-immigration schemes ushered in a new era for the frontier. The pressure on Mexico to contain the flow of migrants more aggressively and an agreement to make Guatemala first recipient of deportees for the rest of Central America led to the militarisation of parts of the border. On the Central American side of the Suchiate, Trump was met with comfortable silence: none of the three presidents of the northern triangle of Central America – from which 90 per cent of the migrants crossing the border into Mexico hail – has publicly protested the US and Mexican governments' pact to effectively install the first line of the northern wall in this strip of land to the south.

lack of interest there in the southern border: an inaccessible boundary that has no cities, only towns, villages and settlements. It is not represented by governors but rather by mayors, community leaders, soldiers, peasants and coyotes. To understand it properly one needs to get lost down its dirt roads.

The border is 1,138 kilometres long and is marked by the Suchiate River as it flows west into the Pacific and the Usumacinta River, which crosses the border between Guatemala and Mexico on its way to the Gulf. The closer one gets to the Caribbean, the more it is blurred by the Guatemalan jungle. It has an intricate mountain topography, much of which is difficult to reach. Some of its municipalities have their own language and others their own laws of silence. Many of the communities that have suffered from the greatest neglect – and oppression – by the Guatemalan state, such as the Kekchi and Kaqchikel, are increasingly seeking refuge in the most

The construction of the Tren Maya, with which President Andrés Manuel López Obrador hopes to connect Cancún to Palenque via Tenosique, also promises to transform the region. In both cases, the impacts of the new policies are uncertain not just in terms of the ecology of the area but also the migratory, labour and criminal ecosystems of this part of the American continent. The southern border of Mexico is a large, rapidly changing unknown.

'Known here as "bombing", the technique involves those on the planes sending coordinates to people on the ground, and the speedboats immediately heading over.'

→ world, the motor of an industry that accounts for almost 16 per cent of Mexico's GDP. The Caribbean – along with the trade winds that connect it all – is also a way of life for Xcalak, 412 kilometres away from all that. At the southern end of the state of Quintana Roo, two hours from Chetumal, Xcalak is a spectacular village of palm trees, turquoise waters, two lighthouses and a lagoon. Its urban planning is limited to three streets of sand running parallel to the sea, and three more that cut across them – but if you had to paint a picture of paradise, you'd have to include this community of three hundred inhabitants where almost everyone is related and knows each other by their nickname.

Its beaches are also the final destination for anything valuable that falls into the Atlantic – more often than not the cocaine dropped by Colombian planes, a technique known here as 'bombing'. Those on the planes send coordinates to people on the ground, and the speedboats immediately head over. They don't always have time to fish out the entire load, and the bundles that get lost can appear days later, wrapped in brown tape, bobbing along on the water, stuck on the seashore or tangled up in the mangroves. Sometimes the bricks are thrown out of the speedboats arriving from nearby islands as attempts are made to erase all evidence and gain speed as they flee from the patrol boats, their cargo tossed into the sea.

Christopher Columbus would never have reached America were it not for the trade winds, those steady breezes caused by the Earth's rotation that enable smooth sailing to the other side of the ocean and are recreated in the Caribbean. Thanks to these winds, it makes no difference which part of this sea you chuck anything into – sooner or later it will most likely end up in Xcalak. In the stretch of gulfweed that Don Luis looks after, for example, a Haitian doll has appeared as well as a bottle from the Dominican Republic and a piece of wood with African detailing.

'In this village beachcombing is a profession we teach the young as one would teach them to fish,' Don Luis explains. 'What else can you teach your children if you've devoted your whole life to fishing or selling coconuts, and from one day to the next your neighbour builds himself a house or shows up with a new truck? Here, young people are the first to learn that the future doesn't lie in working but in searching for, finding and buying a speedboat to keep combing for more. It can be marijuana one day, but maybe a year or two later you'll find the cocaine that will pull you out of poverty.'

On one occasion Don Luis had to leave for a few days to visit the city. When he returned to Xcalak no one had to tell him that a cargo had dropped in his absence. 'I began to hear of someone who hired a band, someone else who treated the whole village to beer, one more who showed up with a new motorbike,' he recalls.

*

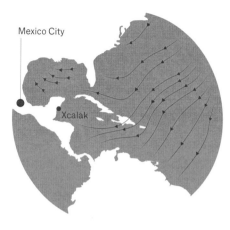

Mexico City

Xcalak

ban on capturing them in Xcalak, so he dives in Belizean waters where there is less vigilance. And few guys are capable of doing it like he does. He free dives six metres deep at night but leaves the boat's engine running in case he has to leave sooner than planned. As he returns to the surface he spins around with his torch, casting light about him in case any sharks appear.

When he remembers last night's 'episode', you can tell that what tickles him most is that he is able to steal from right under the Belizeans' noses – 'But watch out! They shoot with real bullets,' he says with a languid, marijuana-fuelled laugh, talking about the police from the country next door. So today El Guanaco sticks his oar into the water lazily while keeping his eyes on the flotsam. 'It's time to *paquetear*; it's the poor man's lottery,' he laughs again. 'You never know when the brick that will change your life will turn up.' *Paquetear* – packaging, the tireless search for drugs in the sea, and the second homegrown word I jot down in my notebook.

El Guanaco was one of those running past Don Luis's house fleeing the Belizean police the day before we met. It was the dead of the night when Don Luis heard his Yamaha cutting through the bay. El Guanaco is a tough, cagey guy who smokes marijuana non-stop. His nickname suggests correctly that he was born in El Salvador, and, at thirty-three, he has lived more lives than I have space to describe. He says he left San Salvador when the gangs were about to kill him. He fled to Belize, where he worked in the fields belonging to the Mennonites, the ultraconservative Christians who live on the border, until he decided to hide out in Xcalak, the last place where anyone would ask about him.

El Guanaco is athletic and brown skinned and has several tattoos on his chest and back. But today he is tired after the previous night's escapades as he fled with his lobster catch. There is a

As he uses his oar gondolier-style, El Guanaco remembers the day five years before when he found a beautiful package of cocaine. 'It was there, right in front of me,' he says as he points to a patch of sea that is as blue and crystal clear as you'll find anywhere. 'There were three of us, and we found twenty-five kilos, which we split. I got a million pesos [$50,000]; I'd never seen so much money in one go. With that I furnished my house, I bought a motorbike for myself and one for my wife ...' he recalls. 'Normally people go nuts and burn through their money, but I've experienced deprivation and didn't do that. In the end, the money lasted under a year.'

Other than the winds, the new ally of the Caribbean's waste pickers, or *pepenadores*, is gulfweed, which leaves a dense

Above: A huge seizure of 105 tonnes of marijuana and cocaine
at the border between Mexico and California after a clash
between the army and narcos.
Opposite: A soldier keeps guard during the incineration
of confiscated marijuana and cocaine destined for the US.

THE PASSENGER   Jacobo García

The Cocaine that Washes in from the Sea

mantle of vegetation on the seashore that makes the place ugly, damages coral, leaves the fish without oxygen and frightens away tourists. The algae spreading throughout the Caribbean is a concern for Mexico, Panama, the Dominican Republic and Florida but not for those who take advantage of the currents. 'The movement of the masses of gulfweed shows us where the current is going and helps us work out where on the shore the packages might appear,' he says.

El Guanaco received quite a few blows two weeks ago. One can infer from his raw knuckles that he defended himself as well as he could, but it was a beating in every sense of the word. Ten people, including the mayor, kicked him until they had given him a good hiding, and, from what he leaves out of his tale, you get the feeling that he'd tried to be too clever by half. He was working for one of the local drug lords – in other words, charging for beach-combing and for searching the sea for bricks, getting paid up front as he used the speedboat and wasted fuel – but he left that boss and began working for a different one.

*

'Cocaine? Crack? Marijuana?' The tattooed grocer's sales patter leaves no room for doubt as I ask for a six-pack of beer.

In a handful of shops in the village, besides beer they sell 'wet' cocaine – fished out from the sea – at five dollars a bag the size of a fingernail. You can get a similar amount of crack for much less.

In Xcalak the local recipe isn't for seabream in garlic sauce, it's how to cook the damp cocaine that washes in from the sea, a process that the brown-skinned young man explains to me as he sits on a motorbike with a gallon of fuel between his feet. 'You place everything on the stove in a big pot and cook it slowly. You have to

The sargassum that the currents wash up on the beaches of Xcalak also arrives in Tulum, a little under three hundred kilometres to the north. The capital of eco-chic tourism is one of the areas worst affected by the invasion of seaweed, which is harmless to humans and provides shelter and food for many migratory species but has the unfortunate effect of turning the water brown – thus ruining any photos destined for Instagram – not to mention the stench. But the seaweed is only one of Tulum's problems, alongside the precarious state of its infrastructure, over-enthusiastic real-estate agents and, for a few nostalgic diehards, an overabundance of DJs. As recently as the 1990s Tulum was little more than a few souvenir shops near the archaeological ruins and the odd *cabaña* on the beach. Nowadays, having zipped through the classic stages in the evolution of a hip destination at record speed – the arrival of backpackers, followed in quick succession by hippies, richer hippies, yoga teachers, influencers, celebrities, Michelin-starred chefs and, finally, stag and hen parties – it is home to 50,000 people and a 'tourist zone' with around a hundred hotels, even though electricity only arrived in 2020 (despite which the throb of generators hasn't been entirely eliminated). The dizzying pace of development is anarchic in many respects – with vague or non-existent title deeds and tourism licences – and has created a series of environmental problems, from the lack of sewerage to the destruction of the jungle behind the beach, along with a fierce legal battle that has led to evictions and sometimes violent disputes between real-estate agents with the right contacts and hippies convinced that the sargassum is simply a case of Mother Earth taking her revenge.

'In the space of just twenty-four hours, the kilo of cocaine increases in value from $10,000 in Xcalak to $60,000 in Texas.'

stir constantly, to stop it burning, until all the water has evaporated. Then you place it on a board and you begin to cut the cocaine with a large knife. You start breaking up the lumps with a spoon,' he says. To get crack, you cook the cocaine on a double boiler with baking soda. For a kilo fished out of the sea you can make around 200,000 pesos ($10,000).

According to experts, the cartels of Sinaloa, El Golfo and Jalisco Nueva Generación (CJNG) control Cancún, the Riviera Maya and the coastline of Quintana Roo. The Zetas, the cartel that years before spread terror throughout Mexico, has lost power but holds on to small cells in the tourist areas. In the rest of the region, small cartels – almost family sized – have proliferated and participate in the hustle and bustle.

The merchandise leaving Xcalak is taken to Chetumal, and from there it travels northwards or to Cancún – the city with the third highest cocaine consumption in Mexico, according to the National Addictions Survey. In the other direction, a twelve-hour drive along a good highway leads from the capital of Quintana Roo to Veracruz, and it takes around twelve more to reach Brownsville, Texas. In the space of just twenty-four hours, the kilo of cocaine increases in value from $10,000 in Xcalak to $60,000 in Texas.

The remains of two shipwrecks stick out of the water in front of the dock. Many ships with a keel have failed in their attempts to reach Xcalak through the coral reef. There's only one point where it

can be done, with the boat lined up with both lighthouses, a true course of 283° and keeping the dock to the port side.

On the streets of Xcalak you can see evidence of better days – the years when it had as many as three thousand inhabitants, a shipyard and even a dance hall. Back then, vast quantities of sea snails, turtle eggs, lobster and shark were exported from the docks. At the time Xcalak 'was bigger than Chetumal', says Don Melchor, an elderly man of seventy-five whose birth certificate – number two – is proof that he is the oldest man in town. That lasted until 1955, when Hurricane Janet swept it all away and killed a third of the population. 'Back then many people were unloading on the dock. There was even an ice factory and a cinema,' he remembers as he points down an empty street.

Since then, says El Guanaco with a touch of sarcasm, the village lives off three Ps: *paseantes*, *pesca y paquetes* – tourists, fishing and bricks. Tourists come to practise fly fishing or find the most exquisite diving, and they stay in six hotels that employ around forty people and are aimed at international tourists, charging $120 a night. 'But fishing brings in less and less, and tourists don't come, so we have to wait for the sea to make us lucky,' he adds.

'The main activities in this village have always been coconuts, sea snails and lobster,' laments José Miguel Martín – fifty-five years old, the lighthouse keeper – from the very top of the enormous beacon. 'But there are long closed seasons, and when it became a National Park in the

The comparisons between *narcocorrido* music and American gangsta rap, certainly in terms of subject matter, are clear enough. From a musical perspective, however, with their wind and accordion accompaniment, there is nothing tough about these easy-listening ballads following the lives of drug traffickers. The *corrido* is a folk genre that dates back originally to the War of Independence, later becoming hugely popular during the Revolution. The 'narco' version started making inroads in the 1970s, and its success was proportional to the increase in the drug traffickers' power. Initially the songs were merely about underworld activities and drug routes, but with the emergence of such high-profile figures as El Chapo, the lyrics started celebrating the bosses' lifestyles centred on luxury goods and women. It is just a short step from glorification to encouraging emulation, but the songwriters' justification is always the same. In the words of Edgar Quinter, singer in the band Buknas de Culiacán, who featured in Shaul Schwarz's 2013 documentary *Narco Cultura*: 'I do not celebrate the narcos, I just sing about a social reality.' Many ballads could indeed also have a documentary value, but the links between many groups and the drug cartels are proven. There is no shortage of songs that openly celebrate the cartels and glorify the bosses, but, in spite of the criticism, *narcocorridos* have become big hits and have even won Grammys, as illustrated by the career of the Tigres del Norte, whose track on the freeing of El Chapo's son, 'Soy el ratón', has had more than twenty-five million views on YouTube.

year 2000, opportunities became even more limited.' From the lighthouse, just a few metres from the naval barracks, there is a clear view of the comings and goings of motorbikes ridden by teenagers carrying large gas canisters and heading towards the encampments where they spend hours waiting, searching and cooking. 'How can I tell my son not to go when all of his friends are into that?' the lighthouse keeper says with resignation.

Martín and his lighthouse, the port captaincy, the National Commission for Protected Areas (CONANP) and a navy base with ten marines are the only presence the state has in this place. Ironically, the most feared and hated institution in the village isn't the navy but CONANP. Its four delegates may be lacking in means, but they have the enthusiasm to fight for closed seasons and to prevent illegal fishing and to protect the coral reef. Since the municipality has no police force, they report every single illegal activity to the navy. And that, of course, is a big deal. In Xcalak, it's scarier to fish during closed season that to sell on a kilo of cocaine.

According to the Mexican Navy, a plane from Colombia or Venezuela crosses Quintana Roo's air space every two days. General Miguel Ángel Huerta, who is in charge of surveillance of the Caribbean coast, acknowledged to the media that in the first five months of 2019 at least a hundred flights operated by drug cartels had been detected.

*

'In this forgotten paradise crack cocaine costs the same as a bottle of Coke and a bag of potato chips – and the consequences can be found in the burial ground.'

'So, are the village parties big?' I ask El 75.

'Have you heard of Ibiza?' he replies self-importantly, influenced by everything broadcast on MTV and cable television – the most efficient service in a village without running water. For this 24-year-old, the best party in the world is to celebrate either Easter or a neighbour finding a 'package' with a three-day bender and firing shots into the air.

Joaquín's nickname is El 75 because he has a big head and long legs, just like a seventy-five-horsepower engine. The kid tries to be formal in his outings with tourists; he fills the small icebox with water and soft drinks, he carries goggles and flippers, shows them the manta rays and manatees and offers to shift and move the boat's Bimini top sunshade as many times as they need him to. But when there are no tourists he joins his friends 'and sifts through *el recale*'. *El recale* – the algae amassed on the shore – is the third new word I jot down.

Joaquín explains that his uncle found a brick a few years ago, but that stroke of luck ruined his life. 'Since he doesn't know how to read or write he was cheated and given just 70,000 pesos ($3,500). And then he was rash and spent it all on alcohol and other crap that left him even worse off.'

El 75 is deft at handling the GPS, engine and rope, but what he's most ashamed of – what makes him feel truly bad – is that he doesn't know how to use cutlery. With childlike innocence he recalls recently going through the most humiliating moment in his life when, during a family lunch, his relatives realised he didn't know how to hold the fork or use the knife to cut the meat. But he has other skills: he can instantly recognise which criminal organisation any merchandise belongs to, 'depending on whether it's marked with a skull, an AK-47 or a scorpion'.

Xcalak's cemetery – a stretch of sand reclaimed from the mangrove – lies on the outskirts. Every day at sundown Doña Silvia arrives with a machete and a broom, and she sweeps, clips, orders and tidies the place up because she has two children buried there. In this forgotten paradise crack cocaine costs the same as a bottle of Coke and a bag of potato chips – and the consequences can be found in the burial ground. Guatemala records one suicide for every 41,666 people, according to official numbers, but in this village with fewer than one hundred graves there are at least four – all of them young. 'In this grave there's a 22-year-old kid who hanged himself; in that one, a 23-year-old who also hanged himself; there, a 25-year-old who threw himself off an antenna tower, and that other one ...' the woman gestures as she walks among the tombstones in the prettiest, saddest graveyard in the world.

*

I seek out the delegate for Xcalak – a position akin that of a mayor but with fewer powers – for an interview. Nearly a dozen testimonies point towards him and his second-in-command as being the local drug lords in association with their

Four lorries packed with marijuana and cocaine confiscated by the Mexican Army; some packages bear the marks of various drug cartels – a drawing or a sticker – to show ownership. The strapline beneath the figure of Homer Simpson (right), 'Voy de mojarra y que wey', could be interpreted as 'I'm going to get high, dude.'

THE PASSENGER   Jacobo García

43

NOT RECOMMENDED ...

Since Jacobo García's feature was first published in June 2019, things have only got worse in Xcalak. Just two months later the community's delegate, Luis Lorenzo López – the man García was unable to meet – was arrested on suspicion of involvement in the murder of eight people. He was later declared innocent and allowed to return to his position. Things did not turn out so well for Obed Durón Gómez, the mayor of nearby Mahahual, who was interviewed for the article. He was shot dead with a handgun in April 2020. The former police chief was accused of supporting criminal groups, and the main line of inquiry suggests a settling of scores. Violence and disappearances – along with seizures of large quantities of cocaine by the authorities – continued, culminating in a further eight murders in June 2022. According to the investigators, the killings were ordered by the local boss La Pelusa (Peach Fuzz), who holds the monopoly on buying the packages of drugs found on the beach, and the eight victims are thought to have tried to sell their booty to someone else. The problem of 'misgovernment', to coin a euphemism, can also be seen more generally, such as when, in November 2020, a forty-metre section of Xcalak's pier collapsed after a storm surge. The situation in the town is so dangerous for journalists that our photographer was actively discouraged from looking too closely, which is why the photographs accompanying this article were not actually taken in or around Xcalak.

compadre, the mayor of Mahahual, the seat of the municipal government. Rumour has it that they're the ones in charge of buying, equipping and paying for the encampments and the merchandise. The delegate tells me he will be out of town, but he refers me to the deputy delegate, who lives on the edge of the village.

In the shade of the bougainvillea and coconut trees, two friendly families are finishing lunch. They laugh, joke and dig out food from between their teeth with toothpicks. One family is that of deputy delegate Enrique Esteban Valencia and the other is that of the mayor of Mahahual, Obed Durán Gómez. On the chequered tablecloth lie the leftovers of lobster and shrimp, and four municipal policemen stand guard with their weapons hanging around their necks. Although they have no right to a seat or a family meal, they interact in a natural way with the most powerful men in the region – they're at ease.

'What do you propose to do about the gulfweed?' I ask the deputy delegate. 'Do you want the government to send people to clean it up as the hotel owners have requested?'

'They shouldn't come; that's not the answer. No, we don't need anyone coming here,' the deputy delegate answers, clearly not remotely amused by the prospect of crowds of strange people arriving to mess with the village's beaches.

'How do you deal with the drug trafficking problem and the fact that young people are working in this activity?'

'I wouldn't call it an activity. People are free to go wherever they wish. It's not a matter that concerns us – there are authorities for that,' he responds.

'But it's obvious that many people are involved in beachcombing and that your village is an important entry point for drugs,' I say.

'I don't know what you're talking about. It's a subject that doesn't concern us,' responds the mayor, and his *compadre* nods.

'And the encampments we've seen?' I ask.

'I don't know what information you have, but they're not encampments. People need land to live on, and if they don't have any land we have to give it to them,' says the mayor of Mahahual.

'Many people connect you with the purchase of merchandise found at sea.'

'They can say what they want, call me a drug trafficker or whatever, but it's just that we're doing things, and that bothers them,' the deputy delegate protests.

'What things?' I enquire.

'Fighting for our rights so that we're not abandoned any longer, and also against delinquency.'

'Do you want more police? Do you want the presence of the National Guard?' I ask.

'Look, we have our own way of keeping watch,' says Obed Durán, who moved from being chief of police to mayor of Mahahual four months ago. 'And there are three ways of dealing with them [troublemakers]. First, they're given a chance, and we take them to a rehab centre without beating them up or anything. If they do it again, they're given a warning, and if they go too far again … well, a sack of lime will help me avoid many expenses,' he says with a peal of laughter so loud that his *compadre* straightens up and beats the table with his fist.

Evening falls on Xcalak, and a light breeze ruffles the palm trees and rocks the boats. The Latin root of the word *alisio* describes a 'soft and gentle wind', which the British later translated as 'trade wind'. In this case, Xcalak's gift of words has refined the term by combining both meanings. 🐦

Born There

What does it mean to be a speaker of an Indigenous language in Mexico? An Ayuujk-speaking Mixe writer tells the story of how she came to reclaim a written language and an identity that have been suppressed for centuries by Spanish monolingualism.

YASNAYA ELENA A. GIL
Translated by Kit Maude

A woman attending a Frente Ciudadano (Citizens' Front) meeting open to the whole community of Huamuxtitlán in Guerrero state. The community self-defence group was formed a few years ago to protect traditions and land, which were under threat from criminal organisations.

It was only when I moved to the city that I discovered I was 'Indigenous'. Whenever I mention this, whoever I'm speaking to reacts with incredulity. I don't deny that it might be hard to believe, but it's the truth. I grew up in a community in Sierra Norte, Oaxaca, in southern Mexico, in a region known as Mixe, a territory that belongs to one of the many different peoples that anthropologists have designated Mesoamerican. In my maternal tongue, Ayuujk (which means 'the language of the forest'), my community is known as Tukyo'm, and it is surrounded by other Mixe and Zapotec communities in an area of high mountains and steep slopes. At the Sunday markets that we in Mexico call *tianguis* (a word borrowed by Spanish from Náhuatl), I heard other languages, such as Zapotec and Chinantec, for the first time from the lips of traders who had come to sell or exchange their wares or to attend communal festivals. My great-uncle, a traditional prayer-giver, had also learned to read Latin and made me memorise phrases and recite them: *omnia tempus habent*. I think that my great-uncle knew more Latin than Spanish, and in Ayuujk he'd teach me about declension and the different cases: *rosa, rosae, rosam* ... When we went to a funeral, burning candles in hand, we'd sing in Latin and Spanish while older people mixed in phrases from traditional Ayuujk prayers. Even before I had learned Spanish, I knew from my brief and very local experience of life that there were different languages. I'd heard their sounds, even if I didn't know what they meant, because at the time I was monolingual.

Although I had experienced linguistic diversity, my childhood awareness didn't stretch to the history of systems of oppression that had prioritised and classified the languages of the world. I didn't know that my maternal language was considered, like Zapotec and Chinantec, Indigenous while Spanish and Latin weren't. I was oblivious to the ideas associated with such categorisation and the systematic public policy efforts to try to eradicate languages like the one I spoke. At most, I knew that there was a formal, poetic Ayuujk used in rituals, another everyday one and a coarser language that you used in an argument. My mother tongue doesn't have a word equivalent to 'indigenous', and neither do many of the Indigenous languages of the world. What I'd learned was that some people were Ayuujk Jä'äy and some were Akäts, and the Ayuujk Jä'äy were the people of our nation, the Mixe nation, and

YASNAYA ELENA A. GIL is a linguist, translator, researcher and language-rights activist. Her studies focus on endangered languages, including her own mother tongue, Ayuujk. She is the author of numerous essays on Indigenous languages and identity.

A festival celebrated by the Purépecha people around Chéran in Michoacán state. Since 2011 the community has been experimenting with a form of self-government, complete with a community patrol that has replaced the corrupt police.

the Akäts were the first major 'others'; they were all those who weren't Mixe, who spoke Zapotec, Spanish, Latin or English. My language gave me the semantic tools with which to construct 'otherness', but that 'otherness' was built far from the category of 'Indigenous'. I couldn't identify with a word and thus an identity I had no idea existed. So during my early years my identity wasn't defined by the word 'indigenous', although I can't deny that many of the Indigenous policies of the Mexican state did affect my existence and those of all the girls with whom I shared

my games and my childhood. It was just that we didn't know, we didn't know that in other languages ours was considered lesser. I didn't know anything about that because my life was lived almost entirely in Ayuujk, a language that didn't even have a word for 'indigenous'.

All that changed when I entered the education system. Although I still hadn't come across the word 'indigenous', I learned that this new space had no room for my language. Lacking a methodical framework for teaching us Spanish as a second language, the teachers tried to instruct us in reading and writing in a language no one had taught us. This strange linguistic situation meant that, although I could phonetically decipher words written in Spanish, I didn't know what they meant. I could read without reading, I could pronounce the sounds indicated by a given sequence of letters but assigned no meaning to them. Over time some words started to make sense and emerged as graphic islands of meaning in the texts I read slowly and almost always out loud. Little by little I was able to identify patterns and infer more meanings until I had achieved a modest but sufficient reading understanding of Spanish. However, I still couldn't speak the language; that was a process that took several more years.

Outside of school my life continued in Ayuujk; festivals, the market, gatherings, childhood games, my chores, traditional stories and every other aspect of my daily life were conducted in my mother tongue. School had become a walled-off space where it was forbidden to speak Ayuujk. School was a linguistic island where Ayuujk was banned, it was a beacon that broadcast the idea that Spanish was superior to our language. Breaking the rule against using Ayuujk in class resulted in physical punishment: a smacked hand – worse for repeat offenders. Years later, when I started to campaign for linguistic rights, I realised that corporal punishment for speaking an Indigenous language in class had been widespread for decades. I have gathered testimony about different corporal, mental and emotional punishments inflicted upon children who spoke an Indigenous language. Sadly, such practices have not disappeared entirely. Five years ago a school was censured for forcing its students to clean the toilets every time they used their mother tongue, an Oaxacan language, on school premises. I continue to be shocked by the roll-call of punishments: fines for every word of the children's mother tongue uttered, children forced to lift bricks, sent out into the playground to spend hours in the sun, canes whistling through the air before impacting upon skin, hair-pulling, public ridicule, toilet cleaning, hands bound for hours at a time and many more strategies designed to prevent the use of our language during our own education. We bore the scars on our childhood bodies and in our souls, assimilating the idea that Spanish was superior because it was the only language of education. But we didn't know that this was happening because Ayuujk was considered an Indigenous language and Spanish wasn't.

We learned our letters in Spanish. I'll never know what it would have been like to learn the alphabet of my mother tongue. Although years later I learned to read and write in Ayuujk, the sensation of wonder one experiences when one fully understands a written text for the first time took place in a language I couldn't yet speak. It was an act of cognitive violence. Given that it was forbidden to speak Mixe in class, learning to read and write it was inconceivable. We didn't think it was even possible. When I turned eighteen I found out that my mother tongue, the one I spoke every day, had seven vowels. We weren't just forbidden to speak Ayuujk at school, we were denied any information about its grammar and most basic characteristics.

José Saramago, the Portuguese Nobel

'We bore the scars on our childhood bodies and in our souls, assimilating the idea that Spanish was superior because it was the only language of education.'

In the first UN report on the world's Indigenous peoples (2010), numbers were estimated at more than 370 million, 5 per cent of the global population. The idea of joining forces in a transnational movement dates back to the 1970s and the vision of the Canadian Indigenous leader George Manuel, who helped set up the World Council of Indigenous Peoples in 1975. At the time it consisted mainly of representatives from the Americas and Oceania. The struggles and movements for decolonisation during that era turned the spotlight on the demands of subjugated peoples, bolstering initiatives supporting these battles on both local and international levels. The UN was also receptive and established the Working Group on Indigenous Peoples in 1982. Over time, thanks to better funding and a higher profile, the UN body overshadowed Manuel's group, which eventually disbanded in the mid-1990s. In 2008 the UN General Assembly approved the Declaration on the Rights of Indigenous Peoples, which enshrined protection against discrimination, the right to self-determination, to receive adequate compensation and to have control of the resources on their lands. Fair enough, but who are these 'Indigenous peoples'? This is a question that remains open to this day and divides anthropologists and sometimes the people themselves. Perhaps the original inhabitants? But the Masai, one of the most active Indigenous groups, describe themselves as having migrated from Sudan, while the Sami came to northern Europe only after the ancestors of the Scandinavians. The debate could roll on for ever ...

Prize winner, wrote: 'My brain knows me, but I know nothing about it.' You might say something similar about me and my mother tongue during that time. I used it to narrate my world, to communicate my emotions, to reason about my life and to dream, but I knew nothing about it. The knowledge that Spanish has five vowels is so well established that it seems unremarkable. However, such basic information was denied us in our education. The same was true in other fields of knowledge. I learned by heart the names of the rivers of Europe and the capital cities of its major countries but never knew how many consonants there were in my mother tongue. In Ayuujk I learned about maize, about the narrative tradition of the Mixe people, about the uses of certain plants, about different mushrooms and a moral framework to live by. In Ayuujk I learned fundamental knowledge that wasn't codified in writing. At school the textbooks described the Maya and Nahua peoples as

nations of the past who built great civilisations without mentioning that they were peoples who, like mine, still exist today. They also denied us knowledge about our past. If that hadn't happened I would have learned that my language was one of the first in the world ever to be written down and our young minds would have absorbed the ancient spellings used on tablets and inscriptions two thousand years ago.

In time I had to move to the city to continue my studies, and it was there that I learned that I was Indigenous. I was classified as such, and that status was reinforced in many different ways. I know that my experience isn't the same as all those of us who are classified this way. A Mazahua girl who has lived her whole life in Mexico City and accompanies her mother to sell crafts in the streets must have heard the term Indigenous and the insult *india* often in her brief lifetime. There's no way that girl cannot be aware that she's Indigenous, because everything around her repeats and emphasises that that is what she is. I was able to experience my identity as a Mixe girl and not an Indigenous one because I grew up in our territory, surrounded by other peoples similar to mine, where differences in identity took different forms. I grew up in an area where we were the majority and where our way of life and language were the main conduits of existence.

*

In Mexico the term Indigenous is a politically correct way to describe us. When people want to insult us, they choose Indian. Within the community movement many say they would prefer us to be known as the 'original nations'. The truth is that in all the legal documents in force today in Mexico we are recognised as Indigenous. When I got to the city, that was how people there and in the administrative system started to label me. I didn't identify with the term, and I felt inexpli-

cably uncomfortable when I heard it. For a start, the word erased the identity I had felt before. In my new surroundings barely anyone had heard of the Mixe people, and they pronounced it 'miksay' rather than 'mihay'. I realised in my new situation that the category of Indigenous made no distinction between the many different peoples who live in Mexico, obscuring the actual name of my people, which the concept of being Indigenous rendered irrelevant. What did Mixe women have in common with the Seri women from the north? Why should such different cultures be lumped together into a single category? The same was true of our languages.

My initial reaction was to reject the category. 'I'm Mixe not Indigenous,' I would protest whenever I had the opportunity. 'My language, Ayuujk, is a part of the Mixe-Zoque family. It's not an "Indigenous" language,' I'd explain as often as I could. Some Mixe friends and I even started a social network campaign to try to spell out the distinction. As time passed I came to understand that categories of oppression don't disappear just because they've stopped being named. I learned that the policies implemented by the state to govern the portion of its population it designates as Indigenous still affect my body, my language and territory regardless of whether I have decided to accept that categorisation or not.

Once I saw that the ways in which we are classified do not depend on our will, I tried to understand where the category 'Indigenous' came from. In contrast to what might be assumed, the words 'Indian' and 'Indigenous' do not

'But what are the characteristics shared by the Indigenous peoples of the world? What makes one people Indigenous and another not?'

share etymological roots, in spite of their phonetic similarity. 'Indian' comes ultimately from the Sanskrit name for the river that crosses what are now the countries of Pakistan and India. Everyone knows that Christopher Columbus mistakenly thought he'd arrived in the Indies and so called the inhabitants of the newly encountered continent Indians. In time Indian took on negative connotations and so became commonly used as a racist slur. Under the Spanish Viceroyalty the crown always referred to our peoples as '*indios*', but that changed with the founding of the Mexican state in the early 19th century. 'Indigenous' comes from Latin, and its current use is very different from its etymological roots. While originally it meant literally 'born there' – so everyone is indigenous to somewhere – now the word is used to describe a set of specific peoples. In different countries and legal frameworks, the category of Indigenous establishes specific differences from other categories. In the case of Mexico, Indigenous is distinct from mestizo. While under the Spanish crown we were Indian, under the Mexican state we are Indigenous. I'm stressing this point in an effort to lend historical context to words now commonly used in Spanish.

But what are the characteristics shared by the Indigenous peoples of the world? What makes one people Indigenous and another not? After learning about the different historical contexts and situations of peoples classed as Indigenous, I believe now more than ever that it is a political category more than a cultural or identity-based one. A people is considered Indigenous when it has been subjected to colonialism but also, during the processes in which the world was divided into the states that now comprise it, when it has been absorbed by one of the roughly two hundred countries (depending on how they are defined) on the globe, an Indigenous people is a stateless nation that has also been colonised. For a long time academics and anthropologists tried to normalise the idea that Indigenous is a cultural category or one of identity. However, no cultural characteristic is shared by all the Indigenous peoples of the world; it is, in fact, a category full of diversity and cultural contrasts. And indigeneity is not solely an aspect of identity; I was able to live a good part of my life without experiencing being Indigenous in this way. Looking back, I also see that 'being Indian' or 'being Indigenous' apply only to a brief part of our history. We have been Mixe, not Indian or Indigenous, for thousands of years. We have only been Indian for five hundred years and Indigenous for two hundred. Awareness of this presents us with the possibility of imagining an alternative future in which we can go back to being Mixe rather than Indian or Indigenous, given that these are categories that were imposed on us as part of the process of colonisation. Little by little I realised that I could accept being part of the category as long as it was useful to me as a banner under which to unite the struggles of the Indigenous peoples of the world instead of a

LANGUAGES OF MEXICO

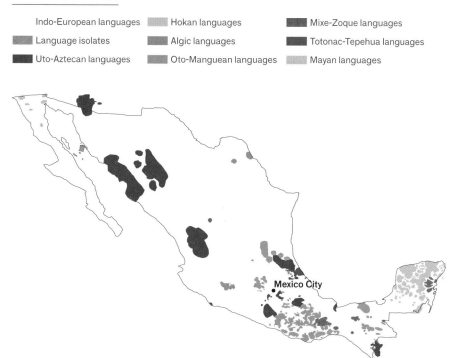

- Indo-European languages
- Language isolates
- Uto-Aztecan languages
- Hokan languages
- Algic languages
- Oto-Manguean languages
- Mixe-Zoque languages
- Totonac-Tepehua languages
- Mayan languages

**Non-Spanish languages
with the most speakers, 2020**

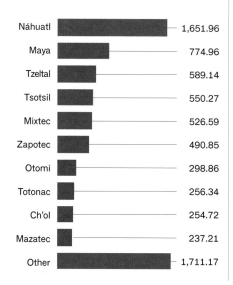

Language	Speakers
Náhuatl	1,651.96
Maya	774.96
Tzeltal	589.14
Tsotsil	550.27
Mixtec	526.59
Zapotec	490.85
Otomi	298.86
Totonac	256.34
Ch'ol	254.72
Mazatec	237.21
Other	1,711.17

Of the 68 Indigenous languages recognised by the Mexican state, 23 are spoken by fewer than 2,000 people and are considered endangered: Kaqchikel, Chichimeca Jonaz, Chocho, Chuj, Cochimí, Cucapá, Guarijío, Ixcateco, Ixil, Jacalteco, Kekchí, Kicapú, Kiliwa, Kumiai, Lacandón, Matlatzinca, Mocho, Paipai, Pápago, Pima, Quiché, Seri and Tlahuica.

Population aged 5+ who speaks an Indigenous language (%), 1930–2020

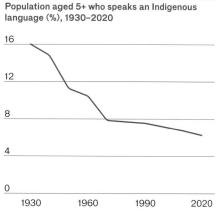

SOURCE: MUTURZIKIN, STATISTA AND INSTITUTO NACIONAL DE LOS PUEBLOS INDÍGENAS (INPI)

Three women on their way to mass
in the church at the former convent
of Cuilápam near Oaxaca.

mechanism by which to obscure the diversity of different peoples, philosophies and cultures from across the planet.

*

Classification of our peoples as Indigenous has also led to the classification of our languages as such. In Mexico, 365 linguistic systems are in use, descended from languages spoken before the colonisers arrived. These systems belong to sixty-eight linguistic groups, which are, in turn, part of eleven language families radically different from one another. Each of these families has entirely different grammatical and diachronic character-

istics. To give an idea of the profound differences between these families of languages, Persian and Spanish are closer (they are both Indo-European languages) than are my mother tongue, Ayuujk, and Zapotec, the language spoken in regions neighbouring my community. Ayuujk belongs to the Mixe-Zoque family, while Zapotec belongs to a family of tone-based languages known as Otomanguean. In addition to all these languages, which are also known as Indo-American, in Mexico other languages related to Spanish are spoken, such as the Plattdeutsch of the Mennonite community, the Romani spoken by the eponymous community and Venetian, which has been spoken in Mexico for more than a hundred years in a community called Chipilo in the state of Puebla. To all these languages we must also add Mexican Sign Language, Mayan

Sign Language and other sign languages in development for a complete picture of the linguistic diversity of the country. Unfortunately this extraordinary wealth of linguistic variety has been divided into two categories for the purposes of public policy: Indigenous languages and Spanish. The other languages related to Spanish aren't mentioned in public discourse, and the major sign languages don't receive much attention either.

At the beginning of the 19th century it is estimated that approximately 70 per cent of the population of the territory we call Mexico today spoke one of the many Indigenous languages. A pressing concern of the recently founded Mexican state was to prohibit the use of these languages, and the stronger the state project became the fewer speakers of Indigenous languages there were. This was especially true after the Mexican Revolution in the early 20th century, when the government initiated a series of policies designed to wipe them out, policies it enforced with particular zeal. It was these policies that shaped my experiences and those of my mother at school. The fact that our mother tongue was considered an enemy of development and progress in Mexico explains the violence visited upon the Indigenous population, and especially its children, in an effort to eradicate our languages. The enterprise has been implemented successfully, given that where once we accounted for 70 per cent of the population, now speakers of Indigenous languages only make up 6.1 per cent. Behind this dramatic fall over a period of less than two hundred years lies the Mexican nationalist mission, the need to create a unified identity. The need for the Mexican state to convince itself that it is one homogenous nation with a shared language, a shared past and a shared destiny means denying what is self-evident, denying reality, a reality that cries out again and again that this is a country of many nations with many different cultures, and this is reflected by multiple linguistic systems. The Mexican state prefers to relate to Indigenous peoples in terms of a glorious past that it can employ for nationalist ends, for tourism or as cultural folklore, while time and again denying their political dimension and their right to autonomy. Realising all this led me to the conclusion that the Indigenous languages of Mexico aren't so much dying out as being killed off by the Mexican state.

The uprising of the Zapatista Army of National Liberation began in 1994, and it was a harsh reminder of a reality that Mexican nationalism had sought to erase from the public discourse. It was a watershed moment that undermined the idea of a monolithic state and brought the plight of Indigenous communities centre stage. Unfortunately, the so-called San Andrés Accords that followed the uprising, by which the constitution would be altered to reconfigure the relationship between the state and Indigenous peoples, were betrayed. Since then, watered-down legal reforms have been implemented in an attempt to bring the matter to a close. However, the truth still tells us otherwise. Schools continue to be strongholds of linguistic oppression, and schemes to introduce bilingual education in Indigenous languages in schools have for the most part failed.

*

After becoming accustomed to these new classifications in the city and adopting a new political identity as an Indigenous person – a category with which I had initially been so uncomfortable – I set out on a return journey. After my initial

Two momentous events took place in Mexico on 1 January 1994. First, NAFTA came into force, throwing open the doors to neoliberalism; and second, the Zapatista Army of National Liberation (EZLN) launched its uprising in Chiapas, a rebellion that entered the collective imagination of the global left, with its charge of symbolism and hope for oppressed peoples in the postmodern era. After three decades of struggles and resistance, the Zapatista movement has lost much of its media power and political relevance. Many Indigenous movements have been inspired by the Zapatistas' revolt – for example, community policing groups in Guerrero and the town that kicked out the corrupt police and politicians, Cherán in Michoacán, and is now governed by its residents. In spite of this, over the years Zapatismo has lost some of its edge, and this was particularly true under the right-wing government of Felipe Calderón when the country was torn apart by state violence passed off as a war between drug traffickers. Much of the Mexican left saw the Zapatistas and their spokesman Subcomandante Marcos (since 2014 rebranded as Subcomandante Galeano) as a political and moral touchstone, but their silence during the most terrible years of political violence, 2006–18, disheartened many supporters. In the 2018 presidential campaign the Zapatistas supported the Indigenous non-candidate María de Jesús Patricio Martínez, aka Marichuy, who was unable to garner sufficient votes to run in the election. The clearest line they have taken in recent years is their staunch opposition to Andrés Manuel López Obrador, the first left-wing president in Mexico's history. (F.M.)

rejection I realised that the categorisation could also be a bond that tied me to the struggle of *all* Indigenous peoples suffering in similar situations. To me Indigenous became a political tool with which to name the oppression suffered by many different peoples on this continent and across the world, and for the first time I felt embraced by hope, the hope of a future in which the category would no longer be required. I suppose that is the journey of people who take words that were previously used to insult us and infuse them with new meaning, full of the power of resistance. I suppose that this is what it means to pick up the stones once thrown to hurt us and use them to build a home, a place from which to defend ourselves. Even though I have found new meaning in the word Indigenous it still seems dangerous to me to use it only as a cultural category, as folklore or as an identity. I refuse to accept that there is such a thing as an Indigenous literature, as if all the poetic expressions of so many different languages had the same status in comparison with Spanish. I refuse to accept that there is one single Indigenous cosmovision and aesthetic just because the colonisers have reduced us to that category. No single cultural or aesthetic characteristic runs through the category of Indigenous; it has always been a political imposition, and it is from that very barricade that we wage our struggle.

The return journey demanded that I return to my language from a new perspective, and as I got to know its grammar I marvelled at my modest but spectacular discoveries: the number of vowels, the nature of the consonants, the types of syllable and the different morphological ways of designating the subject in the Ayuujk language, a language that was at once so familiar and yet unfamiliar to

'Now it's not just the school that has no room for Mixe; little by little it has been expelled from other public spaces, and Ayuujk is increasingly being relegated to the domestic realm.'

me. I finally started to read and write in Ayuujk, and words that had only previously existed for me as phonetic constructions now took graphic form. Poetry and grammar merge in subjective meaning, and from this learning arises a pleasure that should not be denied to speakers of Indigenous languages: the opportunity to reflect on and analyse grammatically one's own language.

Ten years ago I moved back to my community for good. The situation had changed a lot since my childhood; the linguistic displacement had continued, and Ayuujk, which had previously been dominant in my community, was fast losing speakers. Now it's not just the school that has no room for Mixe; little by little it has been expelled from other public spaces, and Ayuujk is increasingly being relegated to the domestic realm. Fortunately the community assembly, the highest power in our system of self-government, still prioritises Ayuujk as its primary language in the intense debates that take place there, but it cannot be denied that children are picking up less and less of our ancient tongue. According to the most recent census, 80 per cent of my community speaks Ayuujk, but on the paths through town one hears it less and less often. This linguistic displacement also affects other Mixe communities, and even though there are more than 130,000 speakers of our language, its medium-term survival is not guaranteed. This is true of other Indigenous languages in a country that once had a multi-lingual society. Spanish monolingualism is spreading everywhere; no Indigenous language reported an increase in speakers in the last census. According to UNESCO, more than half the languages of the world will have disappeared by the end of this century, and I wonder whether, as the decades pass, I will become one of the last speakers of Ayuujk in my community. For now many people are concerned about the situation and are implementing different initiatives to hold back the tide of Spanish, which threatens to wash over everything. A language dies as the result of systematic violence used against its speakers over an extended period of time, and it is that violence that must be stopped; languages are important, but the people who speak them are much more so. Perhaps we have an opportunity to dispel the monolingual dream of the modern nation state, and it is in that hope that we do our work every day to make sure that the nationalist fantasy never becomes a reality.

A Woman Clothed with the Sun

Every year millions of pilgrims visit the Basilica of Our Lady of Guadalupe on the hill in Mexico City where, just a few years after the Spanish conquest, the Virgin appeared – in the guise of both Mary, mother of Jesus, and Tonantzin, the mother of all the gods in the pre-Hispanic belief system – to an Indigenous peasant. With her dual personality, La Guadalupana embodies the Mexican cultural genetic code.

CARMEN BOULLOSA
Translated by Kathryn Phillips-Miles

A statuette of the Virgin of Guadalupe on sale in the huge souvenir market that surrounds the basilica in Mexico City, which is visited by millions of pilgrims every year.

GUADALUPE TODAY

During the course of a single week in mid-December 2022 ten million visitors arrive in Mexico City at a hill known for centuries as the Cerro de Tepeyac (Tepeyac Hill). They have come for the annual pilgrimage to honour the Virgin of Guadalupe, to sing 'Las Mañanitas' (equivalent to 'Happy Birthday') to her on the 491st anniversary of her apparition there. The pilgrims carry statues or images of the Virgin – in their arms, on their shoulders or strapped to their torsos, some larger than they are, others pocket sized. If they're not carrying an image they are wearing one, *la Guadalupana* printed or embroidered on their clothes. The pilgrims are living altars.

Many arrive in the vicinity of the basilica on bicycles or motorbikes, pickup trucks, buses or coaches, their vehicles displaying an image or a statue of the Virgin and decorated with flowers, lights and other symbols; the travellers are chapels on wheels.

As has been the case since 1556, some pilgrims cover sections of the route barefoot, on their knees or on all fours. Most of them pray, sing (accompanied by mariachis, marimbas, violins and guitars) and dance (there is no shortage of feathers and drums, pre-Hispanic style). There are continuous expressions of gratitude to the Virgin, pledges or promises that have already been fulfilled or ones being made for the first time ('I swear by the Virgin that I won't touch a drop of alcohol for six months'). There are plentiful comments such as, 'I've come to give thanks for everything that has been given to me' or 'She works many miracles if you ask her sincerely.' The zeal is palpable. Some pilgrims have made long-distance journeys for forty years or more; for many of the children, I imagine, it will be their first.

I read the papers to catch up with the latest news: following an earth tremor early that morning (measuring six on the Richter scale, according to Mexico City's seismic classification), twelve thousand required medical attention (exhaustion, hypothermia, dehydration, high blood pressure or sores on their feet or knees). They will be allowed (post-pandemic) to sleep around the basilica or in the atrium, on the promenades, in the Capilla del Cerrito, in nearby streets and avenues.

CARMEN BOULLOSA is a Mexican poet, author and playwright whose work focuses on issues of feminism and gender in a Latin American context. She has published nineteen novels and a dozen volumes of poetry, and her works have been translated into ten languages, including English, notably *The Book of Anna*, *Before*, *Texas: The Great Theft*, *Cleopatra Dismounts*, *They're Cows, We're Pigs* and, most recently, *Hatchet* and *The Book of Eve*. Together with Salman Rushdie she co-founded a shelter for persecuted writers in Mexico City. She lives in New York and Mexico.

Just as an anniversary mass was being celebrated for the victims of the 2017 earthquake, the earth began to shake again in a quake measuring 7.4 on the Richter scale. Now there are those who believe there is a curse on 19 September, given that no fewer than three earthquakes have occurred on that day in less than forty years – in 1985, 2017 and 2022 – a coincidence that has also been explored in mathematical calculations to determine the probability of such a repetition, with estimates ranging between a 0.000751 and a 0.00000024 per cent chance. The 1985 quake (8.1 on the Richter scale) killed tens of thousands of people in the Mexico City region, and, according to many historians, the slow progress and inefficiency of the reconstruction was partly responsible for the end of the Institutional Revolutionary Party's long grip on power. Mexico is located in an area of extraordinary seismic activity caused by the fact that no fewer than five tectonic plates – the North American, South American, Caribbean, Cocos and Nazca – meet here. Between 2017 and 2022 there were six powerful earthquakes in Mexico, four of them in September, a month that now has a sinister reputation. Seismic measurements since 1787 have provided some reassurance, though: the most active months are April and December. Recent studies of ancient Aztec codices (or manuscripts) and the accounts written by missionaries, on the other hand, have reconstructed the pattern of earthquakes stretching back centuries that would seem to show that the Trans-Mexican Volcanic Belt (or Sierra Nevada) – a chain of volcanoes stretching 900 kilometres from one coast of Mexico to the other – is an area of much higher seismic risk than previously thought.

The pilgrims form a human carpet with blankets and cardboard boxes and multi-coloured tents.

Many more of the faithful throughout Mexico participate in the festival in their own towns and cities, where the streets and squares are packed. Worship is expressed with a ritualised, frequently festive fervour.

Along the road, other supportive faithful (who live nearer the basilica) have prepared food for the visitors and offer them something to drink before immediately joining the pilgrimage themselves.

The cult of the Virgin of Guadalupe has spread across the border, north of the Río Bravo (there were 38.5 million Mexicans with legal status registered in the USA in 2017, and there were rumoured to be twenty-six million illegal immigrants). In New York a 'torch of Guadalupe' is lit to highlight immigrants' rights; it is organised by the tireless Organización Tepeyac, active since the 1990s. The cult also spanned the oceans – following the trade routes of the 'China Ships' (the legendary 'Manila Galleons', or 'Nao de China'). The vessels that sailed to and fro between Acapulco and Manila and between Veracruz and Cadiz shipped out with Guadalupe on board.

At midnight on 12 December the automatic moving walkway – on which a continuous stream of the faithful passes below her image, eager to see her at a close quarters and spend a few moments at her feet – is turned off. (In 2022, 1,150 per hour passed across the Papal Bridge, which is the main entrance to the basilica.) This is the moment when the traditional birthday song is sung. It takes only three minutes, and, as soon as it ends, mass begins, officiated by forty priests, and the mechanical walkway starts up again carrying its throngs of pilgrims (nobody walks on their

> 'The Spanish-speaking world reflects on the image of Guadalupe – the Mexican flag unfurled at the base of her sacred portrait – and listens to the pop stars.'

own two feet here), eyes fixed on the Holy Mother.

For the past seventy-one years top Mexican pop stars have joined the chorus to sing the praises of the Virgin in the Basilica of Guadalupe. Television channels broadcast the celebration *urbi et orbi*. The Spanish-speaking world reflects on the image of Guadalupe – the Mexican flag unfurled at the base of her sacred portrait – and listens to the pop stars.

Year after year the Guadalupe festival reaffirms the commitment that 'the show must go on'.

HERE WE RELATE HER STORY

The story of the Virgin of Guadalupe is first related in the *Nican Mopohua*, a rich and beautiful literary work composed in the 16th century in the Náhuatl language. Its title is a translation of its opening words 'Here we relate'. The narrative states that in the cold December of 1531, ten years after the fall of Tenochtitlan, on the Cerro de Tepeyac, the Virgin appeared to an Indigenous man, Juan Diego, as he was on his way to mass. The holy apparition asked Juan Diego to take a message to the bishop; she wanted him to build a shrine at the very spot on which she had appeared. In order to persuade the reluctant authorities, the Virgin caused heavily scented Castilian roses to appear where previously only thistles would grow:

The divine gardener,
As a sign of her powers

Chose the most sterile plot
To plant the most noble rose.

As instructed by the Virgin, the humble Juan Diego wrapped the freshly cut flowers in his *tilma*, or cloak, which he wore in front of him, tied at the neck. When Juan Diego placed the roses in front of the bishop, an indelible image of the Virgin of Guadalupe was revealed to have been imprinted on the cloth of the *tilma* – the same one that is still venerated today at the basilica.

Here is another version, by the 17th-century Mexican writer Sor Juana Inés de la Cruz:

Miraculous creator of flowers,
Divine protectress of the Americas,
Who created the Mexican rose
By making Castilian roses blossom.

According to the legend, the image was not made by human hand – it simply appeared as it is, without having been painted – and for this reason it is the most holy portrait in all Christianity. Created by contact with the foreign petals that the Virgin caused to appear suddenly on the rough and rocky Tepeyac, it is composed of colours and forms that, according to experts on religion, were produced from within the cloth itself. A canvas whose fabric, they argue, survives today only by a pure miracle, since its natural fibres are inherently short lived.

The *Nican Mopohua* relates that the

Virgin speaks in Náhuatl, associating herself with the pre-Hispanic cosmogony:

> I am the eternal maiden, Holy Mary, Mother of the True God, Ipalnemohuani, Giver of Life; Teyocoyani, Creator of Mankind; Tloque Nahuaque, Lord of the Near and the Nigh; Ilhuicahua, Master of Heaven; and Tlalticpaque, Master of the Earth.

At the place where she appeared to Juan Diego, on the Cerro del Tepeyac, Indigenous people were at the time still accustomed to making a pilgrimage to celebrate one of their goddesses, Tonantzin, mother of all the gods, and/or Our Holy Mother. They called the Virgin of the most recent apparition Tonantzin Guadalupe.

From the very start Tonantzin Guadalupe was well received by the majority of the population, including the original inhabitants. By 1556 the fervour had spread to the rest of the population of New Spain. Her miracles were plentiful: she saved the life of the son of the city governor, Carbajal, when he lost control of his horse; she contained the plague of 1554; and there were many more examples. Tonantzin Guadalupe protected everyone equally, regardless of social class or place of origin.

She was not well regarded by Franciscans, Augustinians and others who believed that worshipping her was idolatrous – 'a cult that we all feel uncomfortable with', as one contemporary witness wrote. Fray Bernardino de Sahagún affirmed that the cult of Tonantzin Guadalupe seemed to him to be a 'Satanic' invention; he did not like the Tonantzin element at all, especially since the mother goddess was closely connected with another goddess, Cicóatl or Cihuacóatl, who had nothing

A group of worshippers cross the huge public square in front of the old Basilica of Santa María de Guadalupe, built in 1709.

Street vendors and photographers offer their services along the narrow lanes that wind their way up the Cerro de Tepeyac. A souvenir photo wearing a mariachi hat in front of a statue of the Virgin of Guadalupe costs around $5.

to do with motherhood but, in fact, was associated with the devil and, according to Sahagún, had the body of a snake. He relates that among Cicóatl's evil deeds after the fall of Tenochtitlan, during the reign of the second (Indigenous) governor in Tlatelolco, she appeared and devoured a baby in its cradle, and he associates her with 'Eve, who was deceived by the serpent'.

THE IMAGE OF TEPEYAC

The Virgin of Tepeyac is the *mulier amicta sole*, the Virgin of the book of Revelation 12:1, 'clothed with the sun, and the moon under her feet and upon her head a crown of twelve stars'. Surrounded by the sun's rays, with a crescent moon beneath her feet and a crown of twelve stars – which she would lose towards the end of the 18th century, erased so that she could be crowned in accordance with Catholic tradition – the Virgin of Guadalupe has an appearance similar to the medieval image of Mary (of which there were many woodblock reproductions and engravings) that was very popular in Germany and Flanders and by the 16th century had become widespread throughout Christian Europe and which, without doubt, the conquistadors had carried with them.

Following the region's pre-Hispanic tradition, in order to show that she was pregnant (as in the book of Revelation), the Virgin wears a ribbon tied in a black bow just over her stomach. She doesn't seem to be on the point of giving birth to a 'man child', as stated in Revelation

Skulls and skeletons are common images in Mexican culture, from art to cuisine to fashion. For Hollywood, alongside sombreros and drug trafficking, they are almost synonymous with Mexico. Films such as *Coco*, the 2017 Disney hit, or *Spectre*, with its opening sequence in which James Bond joins a skeleton parade through Mexico City, have ensured a global awareness of the Day of the Dead (1–2 November), when many homes set up an altar decorated with flowers, (sugar-paste) skulls and photographs of their deceased along with offerings to attract their spirits based on their dietary preferences, from tequila to mole. The origins of the festival are disputed. It is widely believed in Mexico that it originated in the pre-Columbian world, which saw a circular relationship rather than opposition between life and death, but some anthropologists see the devotion to skulls as a continuation of the Christian veneration of relics, which was then, in the 20th century, overlaid with references to pre-Hispanic cultures in an attempt to rewrite the national identity from an anti-Spanish and anti-American perspective. Another example of syncretism – which has become widespread since the 2000s, often in antithesis to the Virgin of Guadalupe – is the cult of Santa Muerte (literally Saint or Holy Death), a sceptre-wielding hooded skeleton that offers protection to many endeavours, often illegal, in exchange for votive offerings proportional to the scale of assistance required. Her devotees include many drug traffickers but also, in spite of strong opposition from all the major churches, a growing number of ordinary believers searching for refuge from a violent society.

('travailing in birth, and pained to be delivered'), and neither does her composure suggest the possibility that a dragon was going to devour her child shortly after birth. Sor Juana Inés de la Cruz, in a poem dedicated to 'la Morenita', resolves the issue, saying that our Virgin has already defeated the dragon ('whose rebellious head she forced to bow at Patmos') and that, in its place, 'there now treads an angel, a cherub with sovereign intelligence'.

In the *Nican Mopohua* the influence of the ancient Mexicans is more to the fore than in the image with the black ribbon. This beautiful text belongs to the ancient Mexican rhetorical tradition. In contrast, the Virgin's behaviour and tone are in the Mediterranean tradition – not only does her image spring from the roses of Castile, it is 'because, in fact, I am your compassionate mother; I belong to you and to everyone living together in this land as well as all other peoples who love me, call out to me, seek me out and confide in me'.

DECODING – CLOSURE – DECODING

What interests me is the phrase 'compassionate mother' ('*nuestra madrecita compasiva*'). The atmosphere is charged when the Virgin appears and her image is revealed: it had only been ten years since Tenochtitlan had fallen. Among the defeated, chaos, unhappiness, depression and bereavement prevailed – over the human losses in the pandemic, the battle and the destruction of the ceremonial sites and of the great city itself. Among the victors there was fear at the regular uprisings and revolts. There was an urgent need to put together any form of government, to understand the networks of production and tributes and to organise their business activities (or looting, if you prefer that term).

We can take as read the sense of bewilderment and desperation that is confided in a maternal goddess who embraces it all, wraps it in her cloak, exuding compassion unconditionally, smothering expressions of anger and providing a space for the damage to heal. 'The beautiful maiden', as she is called in the *Nican Mopohua*, works to contain and to buffer shocks. In this particular case, one would have thought that, rather than a compassionate embrace, what was needed were muscles to equip her people for restoration, reconstruction and defence. Revitalisation was an urgent need among the defeated. To conceive and forge solutions and tactics for confrontation was an urgent necessity, as were readjustment and the organisation of a status quo that was viable and not overwhelming. As a matter of fact, this *is* proposed in the *Nican Mopohua* as an ideal world where, magically, all is peace and harmony. I quote the opening passage of the story (after the translation into Spanish by Miguel León-Portilla):

> When ten years had passed since the waters, the hill and the city of Mexico had been conquered, arrows and shields had been laid down, and everywhere peace reigned over the different peoples. There was a burgeoning, a blossoming, an opening up of beliefs and knowledge.

Our Virgin was named Tonantzin in reference to the still-present pre-Hispanic goddesses. Energetic and unruly, creators of life and death, they were simultaneously creators and destroyers. Fearsome and powerful, with skirts of serpents, the claws of birds of prey, large, animal bodies, sometimes broken into pieces after fighting with their own children and, even when broken, still moving, swirling, they manifested their fertile power, both creative and destructive, as is the case of the Coyolxauhqui Stone, which one can see in the Museo del Templo Mayor in Mexico City, the monolith's original colours now restored by archaeologists.

Some of those representations of goddesses were festooned with bones. Where an elbow should have been was a jawbone. Knees were replaced by skulls. The empty eye sockets – skeletal eyes – were transformed by death into settings for precious stones. The goddesses provided fertility to the fields, they devoured and gave birth incessantly.

Tonantzin Guadalupe, for her part, the mother of the 'creator of all living things', dressed as the Virgin, spoke comforting words, was presented as deathless (as well as being sexless, clawless and skeletonless). She did not display her bare bones. She had become nothing more

A small selection of
the almost infinite
range of souvenirs
sold in La Villa, the
neighbourhood
around the Basilica de
Guadalupe.

A Woman Clothed with the Sun

> 'Tonantzin Guadalupana is, literally and metaphorically, a projection halfway between the Mediterranean tradition and the unique pre-Hispanic tradition, and is doubly powerful.'

than a dress and a cloak. But she gave comfort to all the *macehuales*, the 'poor little commoners'. She was depicted with her head bowed, looking down and not directly at the viewer, her hands clasped across her breast as if praying; a fold in her clothing suggested she was ready to move towards us, her knee bent slightly as if she were about to genuflect. That knee is no longer a joint denoting death, vitality and action, and it is only in this sense that we can interpret it as static.

The men who worshipped the aforementioned animal goddesses now had to do so as docile little lambs, no longer as Warriors, no longer as Eagle-men (how can we not mention the Eagle-knight in the Museo del Templo Mayor?), no longer as the men who built the great city of Tenochtitlan and the occasional *tzompantli* (walls covered with skulls, which are not merely sculptures but come from the proud heads of defeated enemies).

But she was called Tonantzin, invoking the living memory of the pre-Hispanic gods. So she acted as a source of comfort, provided muscles to enable action.

If she had been just a Virgin of Mediterranean origin, the warriors under her protective cloak would have become nothing more than Juan Diegos on their way to mass, kind and obliging little people, turned into little children dominated by the divine Virgin as she engaged in a dialogue dripping with tenderness: 'Are you not under my care and protection?' The former warriors disappear with her apparition and cult; they are pacified and live under the Virgin's protection, a metaphorical emasculation of the Indigenous population.

It is not an act of cruelty. The Virgin engages in a homely and intimate relationship with the defenceless, obedient '*indito*' ('little Indian'): 'Am I not the source of your happiness?' says the *Nican Mopohua*. Here is the *mulier amicta sole*, a long way away from the dangerous vitality of the sun. Because the sun, truly, is also devastation. But the local goddesses, with their ferocity and ability to generate life and death, are not dead.

That Virgin Mother in whose womb a Son has appeared who is not the product of sexual activity, the neutral, divine protector – emasculator – is she a symbolic negation of femininity? When she says goodbye to her ferocity, is she also saying goodbye to her clitoris and declaring an end to pleasure? Is the subtext 'My dears, it's all over. We are poor insignificant women on the fringes of a vast empire far across the ocean'? Although a mood of negation is detected (Ah, that knee! That assumption of virginity! That Catholic dislike of carnal pleasure!) there is also a sigh of relief: she appeared not to a female but to a male. And it was men who discussed and agreed the construction of her shrine. For the women, now proud Mexican women (we call them *luchonas*, single women and mothers who fight to get by), worthy heirs to the skirts of serpents, it is important to spell it out clearly: the best of Mexico has been built on our shoulders, despite the models of virginal tenderness; we Mexican women devour the world; we are worthy daughters of Tlaltecutli and Coyolxauhqui, the

THE PASSENGER   Carmen Boullosa

'*¡Mexicanos!*' shouts the president from the balcony of the National Palace overlooking the Zócalo, Mexico City's main square. '*¡Vivan los héroes que nos dieron patria!* Long live the heroes who gave us our homeland,' he continues before reciting the names of the revolutionary pantheon: Hidalgo, Morelos, Josefa Ortiz de Domínguez, Allende ... Each name is followed by a chorus of '*¡Viva!*' by some half a million people gathered in the square. The occasion is the eve of Independence Day, and they are celebrating the *Grito de Dolores*, the Cry of Dolores. On 16 September 1810 a parish priest, Don Miguel Hidalgo y Costilla, gathered the people by ringing the bells of his church in Dolores Hidalgo and, holding a banner of the Virgin of Guadalupe, called on his parishioners to rise up, shouting '*Long live the Virgin of Guadalupe! Long live Spanish America! Down with bad government!*' It is not at all clear whether Hidalgo wanted independence from Spain, however; he probably only had an issue with the viceroy. Even today, the tradition of the *grito* lends itself to variations on a theme. Many presidents give the ceremony their personal touch, adding names to the list depending on their political preferences: Benito Juárez and Lázaro Cárdenas are always appreciated, and every so often you hear 'Long live democracy' (which would have horrified Father Hidalgo). Vicente Fox introduced the grammatically more inclusive '*mexicanos y mexicanas*', while Peña Nieto added the victims of the 2017 earthquake to the list. In 2020 AMLO was forced to celebrate the *grito* in front of just 500 people observing social distancing. But, come what may, the last lines never change: '*¡Viva México! ¡Viva México! ¡Viva México!*'

goddesses with skirts of serpents. And we are mothers and not virgins by any stretch of the imagination.

Tonantzin Guadalupana is, literally and metaphorically, a projection halfway between the Mediterranean tradition and the unique pre-Hispanic tradition and is doubly powerful: she is the mother of the recently defeated, with their valley, their mountains, their heaven, their world, a magnificent and beautiful Virgin who, with her virginal presence, offers herself as a protector of the Indigenous people who have no scope for action. For construction. For erection.

INDEPENDENCE

The dark-skinned Virgin is now the embodiment, the physical symbol, of identification with the new nation. She is now called Guadalupe, but never has she been more like Tonantzin, her image emblazoned on banners leading the first battles for independence, the struggles to cast off the European yoke (it was the Napoleonic one rather than the Spanish one that broke the camel's back).

Under the leadership of Miguel Hidalgo an indiscriminate massacre perpetrated by followers of the Virgin took place in the city of Guanajuato in 1810, and when it seemed that they were on the point of storming Mexico City (which didn't happen) there was a mass mobilisation of women. One pamphlet, written, promoted and financed by a woman, Ana María Iraeta Ganuza, and signed by the Patriotas Marianas (the Patriotic Devotees of Mary), affirms the intention to repair the image of the Virgin Mary, distancing her from bloodshed, restoring her bountiful identity, removing her bloodthirsty traits. According to some sources two and a half thousand women joined the Patriotas Marianas (other sources claim it was six

Worshippers move slowly along a moving walkway with their eyes fixed on the image of the Virgin of Guadalupe displayed in the basilica.

thousand). They identified with the Mediterranean Virgin of Los Remedios. They sewed and embroidered her image to be carried as a banner by the royalist soldiers fighting for Fernando VII – and for the chastity and kindness of the Virgin.

The War of Independence was also a war between two Virgins: the Virgin of Tonantzin Guadalupe and the Virgin of Los Remedios. Disappointingly, once Mexico won its independence, Guadalupe no longer led the battle; it was Remedios who won the day.

With no hesitation, however, the Patriotas Marianas also embraced the cult of Guadalupe. They joined in the independence victory celebrations enthusiastically, welcomed the entrance of the Army of the Three Guarantees and the foundation of the new Mexican Empire and restored the cult of the Virgin of Guadalupe. The aforementioned Ana María Iraeta Ganuza, widow of a judge, played a principal role at the court of Iturbide, the new emperor; her uncle, Isidro Icaza, had been one of the signatories of the Act of Independence. Neither of them had children. I am their niece, seven and eight times (respectively) removed. I am not a Marian, but I am, like most Mexicans, '*Guadalupana*'.

BACK TO TODAY

The Virgin requested from Juan Diego 'a little church' in order to protect us all and so that we could worship her, and now she has a basilica, a 1970s architectural gem. Strong and imposing, circular in form like an ancient goddess who, tired

> 'One could not begin to understand Mexico without an understanding of the cult of Guadalupe; it embodies our decoding, our cultural genetic code.'

of gyrating, takes a rest to generate from that spot her creative light, gathering every one of her followers. This ultimate monument to the Virgin of Guadalupe was designed and constructed by Pedro Ramírez Vázquez, the same architect who built Mexico City's National Museum of Anthropology in which so many treasures from the pre-Hispanic period are preserved, keeping them ever-present; it is where I learned, when I saw the goddess with the skirt of serpents, how to appreciate a different form of art, her lopsided body, her monstrous beauty. Modern and defiant, provocative and new, unique, it also evokes the past.

There could be no better basilica for Tonantzin Guadalupe. Syncretism, substitute religion, a religion in which different cultures detonate divergent identities with one single passion. Does its strength come from being a product of different cultures? How can we get to the bottom of its power of attraction?

One could not begin to understand Mexico without an understanding of the cult of Guadalupe; it embodies our decoding, our cultural genetic code.

In 2022 a group of dancers – who came from Ecatepec, now a suburb of Mexico City – arrived at the Cerro de Tepeyac to sing and dance to the Virgin. Their heads bore enormous plumes, and their painted faces and their black-and-white clothes imitated a black-and-white illustration of the ancient goddesses: the white skulls on their joints, the bare bones … The Virgin of Guadalupe is truly miraculous; her memory has not faded, and she still provides us with our energy; she is the embodiment of Mexican stubbornness that is problematic but is also protective; occasionally, short of breath, she stops and takes shelter under a cloak that calls out to us in the diminutive, for we are her children.

For my part, although I am not a Catholic, when I hear the words 'laaa Guadaaaalupanaaa, sobre el Teepeeeyac', especially if they are tinged with the intonation and accent of the Indigenous traditions, I am filled with emotion. In 1962, when we spent a year as a missionary family in an Otomí region of Mexico, my mother wept when she heard the ceremonial lament of the 'Marías', the Indigenous women who came down from the hills to celebrate the Virgin, not dressed in Western clothing, their skirts hiding their feet, which had tramped the muddy roads with no shoes because they did not have any.

It was a moving chorus, not at all Western-sounding. The Virgin of Guadalupe at that moment was in large part the ancient goddess Tonantzin, even though the words of the song ran 'in the sky one beautiful morning laaa Guadaalupaaana, la Guadalupana facing the Teepeeyac'. Now I also cannot contain myself when I hear that song and I see the pilgrims coming from regions in which Tonantzin is still alive. I let loose my emotions, 'my heart undone in my hands' (I twist Sor Juana's verse). 🐦

Final Stop: Tijuana

Life in Tijuana is all about the border, and the city clings to it while reaching out to San Diego, its far-from-identical American twin. Tijuana's commuters see only the traffic queues, but for many migrants the city has become a temporary refuge, the final stop on their journey.

FEDERICO MASTROGIOVANNI
Translated by Alan Thawley

The imposing wall that separates Mexico (on the right) from the USA runs alongside the road leading from Tijuana to the coast.

ZONA NORTE, TIJUANA

A man sorts with both hands through the objects piled up on a plastic tarpaulin. He discards the phone charger with the irretrievably tangled cable, passes over the air-con remote control and pink Hello Kitty torch, weighs up an obsolete digital camera and tries unsuccessfully to turn it on, then sets it to one side. Finally, he asks for the price of a USB memory stick but does not buy it. Without looking at the seller he goes past a stall offering counterfeit trainers and starts to rummage again. A moment later the man is swallowed up by the crowds thronging the street market in Tijuana's Zona Norte and disappears from view.

If the world were populated by cyborgs combining organic body parts with mechanical devices, in the style of *Blade Runner* or *Battle Angel Alita*, I would definitely head to Tijuana in the hunt for spare parts. Of course, the branded versions would probably be on sale in cyborg boutiques in Paris, perhaps manufactured in Geneva or San Francisco, but the place to find the contraband spares, modified upgrades and stolen organs – like the black-market eye transplant in Steven Spielberg's *Minority Report* – would be the cyberpunk city just next door to the little green Californian gardens of San Diego.

Unlike its northern neighbour, Tijuana is an ugly city, devoid of any kind of greenery.

But rather than pirated microchips to install under my skin, I am looking for somewhere to get my beard trimmed. I've been told that the best barbers in the Zona Norte are Haitians and that they ply their trade on the street.

When you say Zona Norte, what you mean is next to the border, up against the wall. Because Tijuana looks northwards. The city is squashed up against the borderline in the north and expands where it can, where there is space: to the south and to the east, because to the west, beyond Playas de Tijuana, you hit the Pacific Ocean. You just need to look at a map to see how the city hugs the border, or, as they call it here, *la línea*.

It really is a line. Thin, constructed of rusty metal, running eastwards for miles towards the desert.

Tijuana clings to the border because it lives for its twin city and twin country. A non-identical twin.

FEDERICO MASTROGIOVANNI is an Italian journalist based in Mexico. He has followed the journeys undertaken by migrants travelling through Mexico and Central America as they make their way towards the United States, and is the author of *Ni vivos ni muertos* (2015) about enforced disappearances in Mexico, *El asesino que no seremos* (2017), the biography of a former Mexican gangster from Los Angeles, and *Aquí acaba la patria* (2021), a journey through space and time that explores the ideas of homeland, migration and borders.

Top: A group of migrants waiting for a meal at the Padre Chava canteen run by the church and a number of local NGOs in Zona Norte, Tijuana.
Bottom: A bullfight in the area known as Playas de Tijuana.

Nuisance Neighbours

Two Centuries of Mexican–US Relations

Translated by Alan Thawley

1810–21

While the Mexicans are fighting for independence, Spain and the USA resolve old territorial disputes by defining the borders of the Viceroyalty of New Spain in the Adams–Onís Treaty of 1819: the USA gives up Texas and gains Florida. In 1821 Mexico achieves independence from Spain.

1835–6

Migration is at the root of the first dispute. In 1830 Mexico bans immigration into Texas from the USA in an attempt to stem the influx of English-speaking settlers. Mexico's president-dictator, Antonio López de Santa Anna (a hero of the War of Independence), abolishes slavery and applies customs duties. In 1836, however, while on a military expedition to Texas, Santa Anna is captured and forced to recognise Texan independence.

1845–8

Texas joins the USA, and Mexico suspends diplomatic relations. The US president James K. Polk asks to buy California and New Mexico. Mexico refuses, and Polk sends in the troops, leading to a large-scale invasion, the Mexican–American War, known in Mexico as the United States Intervention in Mexico. After the capital is taken Mexico recognises the Río Bravo/Rio Grande as the new border following the Treaty of Guadalupe Hidalgo, thus losing around a half of its territory but receiving financial compensation in exchange.

1853–5

The USA buys a region covering 76,800 square kilometres along the Mesilla Valley to build a railway in the so-called Gadsden Purchase, marking the final adjustment to the border between the two countries. Accused of selling off national assets too cheaply, Santa Anna is overthrown in the Revolution of Ayutla.

1861–7

In 1861, after three years of civil war (the Reform War), Benito Juárez, heading a liberal government, becomes the first Indigenous president in the Americas. Conservatives call on France's Napoleon III for help, and while the USA is caught up in its own civil war he invades the country and installs Prince Maximilian of Habsburg as puppet emperor. When the US Civil War ends, the USA for once stands with Mexico in support of the republic, which manages to drive out the French.

1876–1909

During the Porfiriato, the long dictatorship of Porfirio Díaz (who is credited with the phrase 'Poor Mexico! So far from God and so close to the United States'), the Mexican government encourages foreign investments under the slogan 'order and progress'. US capital builds railways, establishes the textile industry and develops commercial agriculture and mineral extraction, later followed by oil. Many Indigenous communities lose their lands and end up working as labourers on the large haciendas (agricultural estates). The two countries' armies join forces in the wars against Geronimo's Apaches.

1910–20

During the Mexican Revolution Washington aligns with whichever faction that promises to protect US interests. The US ambassador, Henry Lane Wilson, helps to organise the coup in which Francisco Madero, the president elected following the overthrow of Porfirio Díaz, is assassinated. US troops intervene directly on two occasions, in the occupation of Veracruz in 1914 and in the failed attempt to capture the revolutionary general Pancho Villa. When the USA enters the First World War the government of General Venustiano Carranza remains neutral, earning itself coveted recognition from the USA. Over the decade of revolutionary unrest almost 900,000 Mexicans seek refuge north of the Río Bravo.

1920–37

With the election of General Álvaro Obregón in 1920 the revolutionary era in Mexico comes to an end, but the USA doesn't recognise the new government until 1923 and only after Obregón promises not to expropriate the US oil companies operating in the country. The US Border Patrol is established in 1924. While Mexico is led by a series of former revolutionary generals, the Great Depression encourages the US government to begin a programme of forced repatriation of more than 400,000 Mexicans.

1938–64

In 1938 President Lázaro Cárdenas, another revolutionary general, nationalises the oil industry to create Petróleos Mexicanos, or Pemex. The USA, under Roosevelt's 'Good Neighbor' policy, doesn't oppose the move, partly to keep Mexico on side in the Second World War. Under President Manuel Ávila Camacho relations grow more cordial, with Mexico exporting materials and labour. These are the years of the 'Mexican Miracle', a period of almost three decades of strong economic growth presided over by civilian governments. Hundreds of thousands of US tourists visit Mexico every year, and Acapulco becomes a flourishing beach resort for the international jet set.

1964–71

The first *maquiladoras* – factories employing low-income Mexican workers to assemble goods for the US market – are established along the Mexican–US border. Against the backdrop of the Cold War the USA supports the repressive government of the Institutional Revolutionary Party (PRI) in its twenty-year internal conflict with student groups and left-wing guerrillas known as the Dirty War, which includes tragic episodes such as the Tlatelolco Massacre in which the army kills hundreds of demonstrators ahead of the 1968 Mexico Olympics.

1969–73

President Nixon – without consulting the Mexican government, which is later forced to sign a cooperation agreement – declares a global war on drugs and deploys thousands of agents along the border, obstructing cross-border trade and work for three weeks. The Drug Enforcement Administration (DEA) is established in 1973.

1976–85

The discovery of large oil reserves in the Gulf of Mexico in 1976 leads indirectly to a financial crisis when the price of crude collapses in 1982. Mexico defaults on its payments, and the USA intervenes to negotiate debt reduction in exchange for reforms to open up the economy. Millions of Mexicans emigrate every year to the USA, which is described by President Reagan as 'an invasion'. Following the murder of a DEA agent in Mexico in 1985 Washington adopts an increasingly unilateral anti-drugs strategy.

1992–6

Mexico, the USA and Canada sign the North American Free Trade Agreement (NAFTA), which comes into force on 1 January 1994. That same day the Zapatista Army of National Liberation begins an armed peasant uprising in Chiapas. Within a year a currency crisis forces Mexico to ask for help from the IMF and the USA and to approve an austerity plan. In 1996 the Mexican Congress amends the constitution to allow its citizens to possess dual nationality, leading to a wave of naturalisation requests in the USA.

1997–2006

President Clinton visits Mexico and promises not to deport illegal immigrants in exchange for a joint strategy targeting drug trafficking, which, according to critics of the agreement, compromises Mexican sovereignty. Plagued by corruption, the PRI starts to lose its grip on power, and in the instability the drug cartels gain influence as they fight among themselves to establish new political connections and carve out new territories, sending violence levels soaring. President George W. Bush authorises the construction of more than a thousand kilometres of new fencing along the border.

2006–12

President Felipe Calderón declares the war on drugs, deploying the army around the country. Under the Mérida Initiative the USA supplies funds, assistance, military aircraft, surveillance software and other equipment. This tough approach – and the arrests of a number of cartel bosses – only serves to destabilise the situation further. According to estimates from the Mexican government violence linked to drugs causes at least 60,000 deaths between 2006 and 2012.

2016–19

President Trump describes Mexicans as drug dealers, criminals and rapists, promising to 'build the wall' and get the USA's southern neighbours to pay for it. This is a low point in relations between the two countries: in 2017, 65 per cent of Mexicans have a negative opinion of the USA, and fewer than one in four Americans has a positive image of Mexico. Amid threats of tariffs and retaliation, President Enrique Peña Nieto of the PRI and his successor Andrés Manuel López Obrador comply with the US president's wishes and help to reduce the flow of migrants from Central America. In 2019 Mexico overtakes Canada and China to become the USA's principal trading partner.

2020–2

A new trade agreement, the USMCA, replaces NAFTA, but the DEA's arrest of former Mexican secretary of defence Salvador Cienfuegos risks derailing relations. In 2022 Joe Biden joins the long line of US presidents to have said they want to reset the relationship with Mexico.

Before dawn has even broken queues of cars stretch from *la línea* through the crazy, chaotic thoroughfares of Tijuana, carrying Mexicans across the border so they can get to work on the other side on time. When someone says *el otro lado*, the other side, they are referring not to the afterlife but to the United States, and California in particular. The thousands of people who cross the border every day go to work in offices, shops and restaurants, as waiters, labourers, builders, cooks, dishwashers, gardeners, carers. Many young people go to school or college in San Diego to get a more marketable qualification and to improve their English. Tijuana lives off San Diego.

San Diego, on the other hand, seems to turn its back on the border. The two cities are like two lovers unable to live without one another but locked in a game of desire and rejection. Tijuana reaches out to San Diego, its inhabitants get up at three in the morning, get into their cars at four, cross the border at six and get to work at seven, in their cars with California plates, with dollars in their pockets and wearing caps emblazoned with the names of US baseball or American-football teams: the Padres, LA Chargers or 49ers. The same people return home as the sun goes down, speeding along San Diego's Interstate 5, which will take them into the centre of Tijuana with no need for border checks. The city 'centre' is located in the far north of the city, hugging the border.

San Diego acts as if Tijuana doesn't exist – no matter that thousands of people arrive every day, like the tide, to keep the city's economy afloat with their labour. As soon as you are on the other side, the cyberpunk city disappears from view to be replaced by green lawns, trees, orderly neighbourhoods, street signs and white people.

THE POROUS BORDER

Mexico and the USA are both divided and linked by their 3,141-kilometre shared border, more or less the distance from Paris to Ankara. More than 3,000 kilometres of desert, mountains, rivers, valleys and, in places, a wall. One of the world's most high-profile and frequently crossed borders marks the unbreakable union between two countries that have never really been independent of one another. The economies of Mexico and the USA are linked by a historically co-dependent relationship. During the revolutionary era US interests were mostly about the production and transport of oil, but, over the years, reciprocally advantageous manufacturing relationships have grown stronger. Mexico's *maquiladoras* offer US companies the opportunity to relocate production and assembly south of the Río Bravo/ Rio Grande, providing work to a vast lower-cost labour force, specialised or otherwise, which produces the goods that are then transported back north on a daily basis. Currently almost forty million people in the USA were either born in Mexico or claim Mexican heritage, half of whom live in the border states – in California, Texas and Arizona alone there are more than twenty-one million – and who contribute to the economy and wellbeing of the United States. Mexico would be unimaginable without the US economy and without the remittances that in 2022 stood at more than $58 billion, just as the US economy could not operate without its special relationship with workers in Mexico and the millions of immigrants. (F.M.)

A mural of a Haitian woman painted by the artists Ariana Escudero and Miguel Paredes at the entrance to the headquarters of Espacio Migrante, a community organisation that fights to protect the rights of migrants in Tijuana.

The Mexican film industry is growing fast and garnering ever more coverage around the world, regaining the status it lost after its golden age in the 1940s and 50s. The phenomenon goes beyond the trio of multi-award-winning directors who have become permanent fixtures in Hollywood: Guillermo del Toro (*The Shape of Water*, *Pinocchio*), Alfonso Cuarón (*Children of Men*, *Gravity*) and Alejandro González Iñárritu (*Amores perros*, *Birdman*). The Mexican industry is also present and well represented at all the world's major international festivals, offering a series of new perspectives and approaches that reach a wide variety of audiences. Narrative films range from the disturbing work of directors such as Carlos Reygadas, Michel Franco and Amat Escalante to stories of everyday life such as those told by Tatiana Huezo, Lila Avilés and David Pablos. But there is another industry in Mexico that challenges the more polished, award-winning productions and is responsible for the B-movies produced in Tijuana for the huge home-video market. Inspired by US, Italian and Asian action movies, the directors of narcofilms – action movies in a similar vein to Hollywood blockbusters but with stories that resonate emotionally with millions of nostalgic immigrants – produce dozens of titles a year on tiny budgets, relying on the abilities of an army of professionals who often work in nearby Los Angeles. The plots of these gritty crime dramas set on the northern border revolve around shootouts, betrayals, explosions and drug trafficking and are hugely popular among Mexicans living in the USA. (F.M.)

My friend Gustavo told me he always goes to Michel, a Haitian who cuts hair on weekends on the Calle Baja California in the Zona Norte street market. It is a Sunday morning in November, and we arrange to meet outside the Santuario de la Virgen de Guadalupe. Gustavo texts me to say he is waiting for me in a *taquería* because he got a bit hungry. I catch up with him as he is polishing off a couple of fish tacos, and we head into the alleyways that form between one stall and the next, covered with coloured plastic sheets. The further north we go the darker the sellers' skins become. Haitians are in the majority in this part of the market.

In 2016 Haitian migrants began to arrive in large numbers, trying to reach the USA overland after yet another natural disaster, this time caused by Hurricane Matthew, which, between late September and early October, killed around a thousand people in the Caribbean country and displaced hundreds of thousands more.

In 2017 the Temporary Protected Status introduced by then US President Donald Trump was suspended, bringing a sudden halt to the distribution of visas. So the Haitians found themselves stuck

'Tijuana is in decline. Even during the golden age of the casinos, nightclubs and affordable vice, it was a place of moral decline.'

in Tijuana, unable to cross the border or return to Haiti. Trapped in a cyberpunk city almost 5,000 kilometres from home.

The border is clearly visible from here, just two blocks away. You can see the rust colour of the metal wall. And behind the wall is the outlet mall Las Americas, where you can buy anything at low prices – but first you have to get to the other side.

Gustavo and I, meanwhile, thread our way through the crowd. Gustavo is an Afro-Colombian, nearly two metres tall, who has the face of an overgrown child and smiling eyes. Together we make a strange pair, attracting curious looks from passers-by.

'I don't understand why everyone thinks I'm Haitian,' Gustavo tells me bitterly.

'Perhaps because you're black and the place is full of Haitians?'

'I'd call that a racist attitude.'

'You really don't see many Afro-Colombians around here. People tend to simplify. It's full of Haitians here. Haitians are black, you're black, so you must be Haitian, too. And in any case, the Haitians talk to you in Creole as well – even *they* take you for a Haitian, not just the Mexicans.'

'Well I think it's obvious I'm Colombian.'

The conversation continues in this vein until we finally get to the barber's.

Even though we are sitting on chairs in the middle of the street, Michel's kiosk is well equipped: a rectangular mirror hanging on one of the walls, which are actually different-coloured tarpaulins, a sort of carpet on the ground, two swivel chairs to accommodate two customers at a time and all the equipment you need for a perfect shave. Next to me sits a young Haitian who looks at me like I'm an alien, white customers being a pretty rare sight around here. Michel tells me that white people don't often come to him for a shave. Gustavo, on the other hand, is a loyal customer who comes every weekend.

'Mexicans don't understand our hair. They don't know how to cut it. I need Haitians or Africans to cut my curls properly.'

The shave takes almost an hour. Each stage is a meticulous process, carried out with a wide range of equipment: scissors, different types of electric shaver and a razor. I feel truly pampered.

When the job is done, in addition to having an impeccable beard, I know more than I did before I sat down. I know that Michel has been here since 2017, that he tried to put himself on the waiting list for an asylum-seeker's visa but was unsuccessful. I know that he is twenty-eight and ended up finding his niche in Tijuana. Not just this street-barber's stall in the Calle Baja California but also a place in Tijuana's Haitian community.

'Of course, I'd prefer to be on the other side, but basically this is a good place to be. There are so many Haitians here.'

And a stone's throw from the barber's a statuesque woman is grilling skewers of chicken. Gustavo and I manage to take three steps before we're sitting down again, this time at a rectangular table covered with a tough red-plastic cloth.

'The *patacones* here are out of this world, like the ones you find in my

THE PASSENGER Federico Mastrogiovanni

country,' says Gustavo as he prepares to bite into a gigantic skewer.

Patacones is the Colombian name. In Haiti they are fried plantains, which accompany many dishes in Creole cuisine, from the Caribbean to Colombia and all across Central America. The chicken is excellent – simple, spicy and delicious – and the *patacones* are irresistible. You want to eat them by the bucketload.

The Zona Norte is a crucial meeting place for a community that has been trapped here through no fault of its own. Overlooking the border, it is the closest that those unable to cross can get to the American Dream.

Avenida Revolución, 'La Revu' for short, a few blocks from the *patacones*, is the thoroughfare that splits the heart of the city in two, leading to a metal archway standing over sixty metres high that from a distance resembles the hollowed-out silhouette of a Space Shuttle about to lift off. The Arco Monumental, a public work commissioned by former mayor Kiko Vega, was designed to welcome tourists in the new millennium, but they only managed to inaugurate it in late 2001. The new millennium had already arrived, and after a few years the tourists stopped coming, because while Tijuana might well be sin city, young Americans have no taste for real danger. So as soon as the city descended into a chaotic mess of violence, murder and disappearances, tourism vanished as well, and the Avenida Revolución was left deserted, along with its enormous bars and nightspots with their gigantic terraces, where, until 2007, before the so-called war on drugs broke out, it was impossible to move, and if you lost your footing you wouldn't fall because they were so packed. The arch is visible from almost everywhere in Tijuana, and even from San Diego it always seems to be staring you down. It is also a huge optical illusion, because you can never work out exactly which way it's facing.

Tijuana is in decline. Even during the golden age of the casinos, nightclubs and affordable vice for young Americans who wanted to feel wild and free, it was a place of moral decline. Tijuana was a den of iniquity before becoming caught up in an extremely violent war. It has always been a transient place, but as soon as the conflict became less violent, in around 2012, it became a place of deportation, the landing point for the undocumented Mexicans and Central Americans who are spat out of the USA. Now it is a waiting room, a place where people wait to be called up to receive asylum.

Tijuana has become the final stop on the line.

LITTLE HAITI

Alejandro Cossío, a photographer friend from Tijuana, gave me directions to Little Haiti. He was quite meticulous, but I still got lost among the dirt roads of the Cañón del Alacrán, Scorpion Canyon. I just cannot find the structure built by the Embajadores de Jesús, the Ambassadors of Jesus, which apparently everybody around here knows but is impossible to locate. The closer I get to my destination, the less sense the directions seem to make.

'When you get to the grey house, you need to follow the road to the right.'

The houses are all grey, I try to argue, somewhat perplexed. And after the bend the potholed road fans out into an endless series of forks. I take the one that seems to be the closest match to the description, but after a long detour I find myself back where I started. If nothing else, the wild goose chase allows me to get a closer look at the neighbourhood.

The Zapatistas of Chiapas and Donald
Trump agree on one thing at least:
NAFTA. The North American Free
Trade Agreement between Mexico,
the USA and Canada was, in the US
president's words, 'the worst trade
deal ever signed'; the Zapatistas
had reached the same conclusion in
1994 when they began their rebellion.
NAFTA forced Mexico to strike out an
article in its constitution that protected
Indigenous land from privatisation,
which had been the real triumph of
Emiliano Zapata's revolution. Trump
had other things in mind, however – the
loss of jobs in the USA and the trade
deficit – and, as he had promised in his
election campaign, he renegotiated the
agreement, although obtaining little
more than a new acronym: USMCA
(the United States–Mexico–Canada
Agreement). In 1994 the Mexicans had
been told that NAFTA would create jobs
and expand the middle class – and it is
true that exports and foreign investment
grew at a dizzying pace – but economic
growth and pay remained stagnant,
and small-scale Mexican agriculture
could not cope with the impact of
subsidised maize from north of the
border. And then there was the collateral
damage: the agreement turned out to
be an obstacle to the environmental
regulation of industries, in particular
extractive industries, while food imports
from the USA inundated Mexico with
processed food, sugary snacks and
drinks, leading to a transformation
of the diet of many Mexicans that
numerous experts see as the main
cause of rising obesity rates (see 'An
Overweight Country' on page 155). So
the deal did bring some growth ...

The river of cars that that flows through the San
Ysidro border crossing every day; traffic volumes
at the crossing point between Tijuana and San
Diego are the highest in the world.

Unauthorised constructions line the rough slopes of the canyon, one on top of the other, alternating with tin shacks, missing planks of wood and trickles of black water which flow by your feet like little liquid serpents and are no doubt on their way to meet the Styx.

There are people waiting for the bus, which is actually a minibus, their eyes fixed on the glow of their phone screens. Most of the neighbourhood dogs are lounging in the shade of the occasional threadbare tree or walking unchallenged down the middle of the street, increasing the already chaotic traffic.

Finally, after asking what feels like

'The Haitians fought for a place where they could have beds to sleep in and something to eat. And so Little Haiti was born.'

thousands of people, I manage to find the entrance to the Cañón del Alacrán proper.

'It's up there,' I'm told by a woman with the air of someone having to provide the obvious answer to a stupid question. 'You have to follow the road. It'll take you seven minutes at most.'

The 'road' is a muddy slope. After six minutes and forty-three seconds, during which I have to wade across the same black stream twice, avoid two dogs and wave hello to three women with various children and an old man with a wizened face, I reach my destination. At the top of a little hill perched on the slope of the canyon stands an imposing structure, at least compared with its surroundings, whitish in colour and occupied by dozens of busy people. The Ambassadors of Jesus Church. Praise the Lord.

Little Haiti is not a neighbourhood of the city of Tijuana inhabited by Haitians, along the lines of Little Italy in New York, for example; it is a temporary accommodation centre for migrants perched amid the shacks in a remote area to the south of the Playas de Tijuana district.

Nidia is a Honduran woman who has been living here for three months with her husband and her two children, Melany and Cristopher. She helps to run the accommodation centre, and she shows me around and explains how it works.

'All new arrivals are registered. They are registered on the system at the church, and here in the dormitories we have a paper register.'

The register is needed so that everyone who arrives is put on the waiting list for an appointment with US immigration officials as a seeker of political asylum. The wait can be months, and the church is one of the places where you can wait your turn without having to live on the streets. There is no charge to stay, but the rules are very strict, and Nidia is one of the church's guests tasked with ensuring those rules are followed. In the communal areas, the bathrooms and dormitories, order and cleanliness rule. There is always someone sweeping the floor or loading clothes into a washing machine. While she chats with me and shows me around, Nidia tells other guests how to put away the bedrolls, what time the next meal is or how to clean the bathrooms.

'Not a leaf moves without your permission. You seem born to lead!'

Nidia looks at me and tries on a severe face before breaking into noisy laughter. 'Yes. Some people like me here, others are afraid of me,' she says, guffawing, 'because I'm very demanding. The fact is that what I expect of them is also asked of me. So, of course, I have to be a bit strict.'

At the entrance to the dormitories is a board listing the jobs to be done, mealtimes, the times of medical and psychological appointments and the rules for coexistence. The first and most important rule is that the church must be looked after from Monday and Friday. Then, in descending order: children are not to be mistreated or smacked; no wearing of indecent clothes; no smoking; no alcoholic drinks; no bad language. Young people are not permitted to have romantic or sexual relationships. It is compulsory to make the beds and clean the floors, bathrooms and communal areas. Finally, guests must help the pastor, Gustavo Banda, with any jobs that need to be carried out for the church, such as brickwork, carpentry, plumbing and anything required for the construction of the new wing of the refuge being built on another slope of the canyon across from the church.

'This place is huge. How many people live here?'

'The number varies. At the moment there are almost nine hundred of us, but sometimes it can be over a thousand.'

Some arrive at the church, register and then disappear. To avoid this, Nidia and the other caretakers constantly check that those who register are really living here and doing the jobs that the pastor requires. This is because there are migrants who only register in order to be included on the immigration service's lists and receive the call.

I have already been here an hour and have yet to see a single Haitian. This place is called Little Haiti because in 2016 there was a big wave of Haitian migrants in Tijuana. But the Haitians are a proud, rebellious people, used to fighting for what they need, so they fought for a place where they could have beds to sleep in and something to eat. And so Little Haiti was born.

I ask Nidia to introduce me to some Haitians I can interview, so she takes me to the church and introduces me to Nani.

Nani is a forty-year-old Haitian woman, here with her two children, the eldest ten and the youngest four, along with her husband, who is currently working as a labourer on the construction of the church's new kitchen. Her Spanish is pretty good, and she speaks fluently, but she didn't learn it here.

'It's because I'm from Belladère on the border with the Dominican Republic.' She has been told the reasons this place is called Little Haiti, and she knows that there is a sort of respect for the Haitians, but she also knows that this sometimes spills over into hostility. 'Because we don't let people walk over us.'

Nani and her family are already on the list for political asylum, but it is very frustrating not to know how long they will be waiting. Admittedly, this is a feeling shared by all the guests at the centre. But Nani is Haitian, and Haitians are not in the habit of putting up with things.

'Nidia was telling me you're treated quite well ...'

'Weeeell ... how can I put it ...? I don't think it's that great.'

Nani straightens her back, her arms folded across her chest, switching between watching her daughter playing a few metres away and looking me in the eye.

'We're grateful to the pastor who took us in, though it's not the way we wanted it to be. Soon I'll have been here four months. We weren't expecting it to take so long to give us asylum, but the time isn't the problem, it's the way we have to live. Because even though we're poor there are some things we can't get used to. We're used to not having much, but not like this. For example, the bathroom where we all wash, the kitchen where we all cook ... Sometimes when it's lunchtime we don't even manage to eat. Do you know what I mean?'

I do know what she means. I nod in agreement. She stares at me intently. In silence. She wants to be sure I really have understood.

'And then the dormitories. They're very uncomfortable. We're poor, but this isn't the right way. Sometimes you're disrespected by people you don't even

Top: While waiting for his asylum request to be processed by the US authorities, Daniel works occasionally as a barber at a street market (*tianguis*) in Zona Norte, Tijuana.
Bottom: Labadee Haitian restaurant in central Tijuana is one of the many businesses set up in recent years by members of the city's Haitian community.

know. And then we don't know how long we'll have to stay here.'

The reception centre is at this time home to another sixteen Haitian families who live in the upper part of the building in an area set aside just for them. A few days ago there was a rainstorm, and the area was completely flooded. Nani spent the night, along with all the other residents of the centre, trying to bail the water out of the kitchen and the dormitories with buckets, cleaning and drying so that the kids could have at least a few hours of sleep. In Florida, she says, they have Haitian family members who emigrated there years ago waiting for them.

Nidia comes over to take me back to the entrance. While Nani was talking she was giving me looks that I interpreted as critical. Now she has decided to intervene.

'Well, it could be worse, right? At least we have something.'

Nani looks at her with disdain and does not reply.

DOWNTOWN SAN DIEGO

As soon as you cross the border, leaving Tijuana behind and entering California, the landscape changes drastically and everything looks sunnier. It makes no sense, because Tijuana is literally attached to San Ysidro, an outpost of San Diego. But it is true. Even though San Diego basks in the same sun, in Tijuana it illuminates a different world, a world of chaos, unplanned development, disharmony and ugliness.

Every place changes depending on where you view it from, which is why I decided to cross the border and see what Tijuana looks like from San Diego. And the first thing that happens as I join the traffic on San Diego's Interstate 5 in an electric Chevrolet is that I have the sensation that Tijuana no longer exists.

I have to make an effort to remember that behind me, still only a few hundred metres away, is the chaos of Tijuana. I am also reminded that in Hollywood films, as soon as you cross the Mexican border, you see things through a warm filter, as if Mexico were a dusty place all in shades of yellow. Well, the reality may be somewhat different, but it is true that your eyes can rest a little, and you start to see some green here and there.

The Chevy EV belongs to my friend Alva Méndez, a Mexican from Tijuana who moved to California twenty years ago. She has come with me because I want to meet a friend of hers, José Lobo, a Mexican painter who has been living in San Diego for forty years and observing Tijuana from the USA.

So after the first moment of bewilderment we make our way to call on him at his very modest apartment in University Heights, one of the city's historic residential districts. (There is a stone on the pavement outside José Lobo's house inscribed with the words 'Founded in 1889'.) The area is home to lower-middle-class working people, as he tells me himself after inviting me to take a seat on his extremely soft couch, which I sink into.

In addition to his painting, Maestro Lobo likes to photograph people on the street as examples of the intertwining of cultures that typifies the United States today. He wants to take me around to show me some of the places that bear out his research.

Our first stop is the Cambodian temple Wat Sovannkiri on University Avenue. It genuinely is a building in the Buddhist style, the sort of thing you would imagine in the most obvious of clichés, with pastel-coloured winged angels and terrifying figures of demons holding up an oriental-style roof, set among the low, beige-coloured buildings typical of this part of California. There is not much going on in the temple that day, so we limit ourselves to a stroll around. José Lobo is enthusiastic about the way immigrants can live alongside one another and intermingle in San Diego, giving rise to new ways of belonging.

Two streets away from the Buddhist temple, where University Avenue crosses 50th Street, we enter a small red house, once again with an oriental-style roof, which is home to the Chinese Friendship Association. Inside, two elderly ladies are having a conversation in Chinese and pay no attention at all to our presence. The association's headquarters are full of statuettes of what look to me to be furious deities and red-lacquered furniture. All over the walls are sheets of paper covered in Chinese characters. These are familiar places for the artist, milestones within the everyday geography of a long-time immigrant in search of meaning among other immigrants.

I ask him how he perceives Tijuana from here, and I received this laconic response. 'For fifteen years I went to work every morning in Tijuana. Outbound, all the traffic was on the other carriageway and mine was empty. And on the way back, in the evening, it was the same.

He lived in a contraflow for fifteen years.

That was all. And these days Tijuana has no bearing on his modest existence. The boundaries of his life have narrowed down to fragments of San Diego, a city that changes appearance every day, according to how its migrant population is settling.

One of the two Chinese ladies suddenly gets up and walks purposefully over to me. She takes my hand and starts to scrutinise it, talking to me in Chinese English, which I find completely incomprehensible. I am slightly alarmed by this tiny woman determinedly telling me my fortune. I agree with everything she says. She is sure to be telling me something fundamental, something essential about my life. And I pretend to understand and smile. I thank her. We leave.

A few metres from the entrance – with its large white statue that I take to be a figure of Confucius – is a group of African men. No women, just a dozen men. They are Ethiopian, the artist tells me, and they can be found on this street corner every day, shouting and playing dominoes or cards, perched on makeshift stools. This corner has now become Ethiopia.

But what José Lobo wants to show me is downtown. 'I want you to see with your own eyes the cruel side of this society,' he says.

Back in the car we reach the orderly grid of parallel and perpendicular roads that make up downtown San Diego. The area is covered in tents belonging to the thousands who live on the streets.

We park the car, and next to us a couple lounge on the pavement under two black umbrellas, lying on the ground among the tents. They are watching videos on a mobile phone, cuddling and laughing. As if they were on the beach. As I watch them I hear the silky voice of Frank Sinatra approaching, singing *Fly me to the moon, let me play among the stars, let me see what spring is like on Jupiter and Mars*. I turn to look at the other side of the pavement. To judge from his appearance, skin tone and facial features, the man approaching appears to be Latino. He walks confidently, bare chested, with a black longboard in one hand and a gigantic boombox on his shoulder. This is the source of Sinatra's amplified voice.

'Tijuana is the city that every morning spews out San Diego's workforce and every evening welcomes its children back, tired of their dreams.'

The couple turn to look as well. Then look back at each other, smile and embrace.

At the corner of 14th Street and Imperial Avenue, Francisco, Frank and Manuel look back on their lives.

'We got old,' they tell us in a language that is not their own.

All three are Mexican, all three are over fifty and all three are gay.

In Ciudad Obregón, in the state of Sonora, where Frank was born and grew up, it was not easy to be gay in the 1960s.

'On the corner by my house there used to be transvestite prostitutes. Every so often groups of locals armed with sticks would come and give them a beating. I was terrified. That's one of the reasons I came over to this side.'

Frank has lived in California for fifty years. He is now seventy-three, has an apartment a few metres from this street corner and receives enough pension to survive on. Unlike Francisco and Manuel, Frank took citizenship, with the help of his husband who died a few years ago. But he spends his days sitting here with his friends.

Francisco is a craftsman originally from Puebla, with curly hair and a black moustache. He makes rings and other objects from woven bamboo. He has not been back to Mexico for thirty years because he has no US documentation, so if he left he would not be able to return. He shares his cigarettes with a young white American in his thirties who doesn't speak a word of Spanish, wears sunglasses and lives on the street with Francisco. Manuel doesn't say much, but half an hour after I arrive he gets up from the low wall they are sitting on and disappears. A few minutes later Frank points him out to me, hugging a little tree a few metres away from us under the influence of fentanyl.

'I hang out with them to stop them taking drugs, too, you know? I lived on the street for three years, and I took drugs as well. It's just that it's crawling with dealers round here, and they don't like me getting involved. Manuel, if you let go of the tree it'll fall over! Make sure you hold on!'

We are two blocks away from Petco Park, the stadium where the San Diego Padres baseball team plays. When there is a game on the police clear the whole area, move the homeless out and have the tents on the pavement taken down in order to restore the views in this neighbourhood a stone's throw from the bay. Then, once the game is over, the tents and the homeless return to fill the streets.

These are the failures of a system in which, as Frank puts it, you cannot afford to be vulnerable.

And finally, Tijuana reappears. It was always there, but now it is visible. Tijuana is the city that every morning spews out San Diego's workforce and every evening welcomes its children back, tired of their dreams. Tijuana is the place it is impossible to return to. It is the other side without which the USA is unthinkable.

San Diego tries its hardest to pretend that Tijuana doesn't exist, but Tijuana doesn't need its recognition. 🐦

Underground Tenochtitlan

Translated by Simon Deefholts

There is an assumption that Mexica culture was wiped out completely by the Spanish conquest, but you need only scratch the surface of Mexico City's contemporary street level or delve into the customs, food and language of its inhabitants to realise that the ancient civilisation never died and lives on, there for those who want to find it.

Guadalupe Nettel

Thronce are few extant documents that record what the great city of Tenochtitlan, now called Mexico City, looked like. Perhaps the best known is the letter that Hernán Cortés sent to Emperor Charles V to describe it. He confesses that he is amazed by its size ('as big as Seville or Cordoba') and he affirms that its beauty is comparable only to that of Venice, since it was built over a lagoon and, to move between its numerous islands, the residents would travel by boat along canals. The Mexica, who were called Aztecs in the traditional historiography, were the founders of Mexico-Tenochtitlan, and they were the last Mesoamerican people to create a rich and complex culture encompassing religion, politics, astronomy and the arts. Around the 15th century, in the late post-classical period, the city became the centre of one of the most extensive states in Mesoamerica. Tenochtitlan, the capital of the Mexica Empire, covered the area known today as the Historic Centre of Mexico City and its immediate surroundings. The streets in this part of the city follow the routes of the old canals just as many of the wide avenues, such as Río Becerra, Río Magdalena and Río Churubusco – these days traversed daily by thousands of cars – were built over the principal rivers. These are not dry riverbeds, and their waters still flow underground in the same way as the civilisation that developed on their banks. Although the presence of antiquity is not as evident in Mexico City as in Rome or Athens (since the Spaniards destroyed it almost entirely in order to build on its ruins), it is still there around every corner, and it is possible to find it if we follow the right clues.

This city, like almost all settlements that date back a thousand years or more, is made up of many layers, some deeper than

GUADALUPE NETTEL is an author from Mexico City. She has been awarded a number of prizes, including the Premio Herralde for her 2014 novel *Despues del invierno*, which was published in English as *After the Winter* (2018). Other titles translated into English are *The Body Where I Was Born* (2017), *Bezoar: And Other Unsettling Stories* (2020) and the International Booker 2023-shortlisted *Still Born* (2022). She is the editor of *Revista de la Universidad de México*.

others, and I am not just referring to the archaeology. Perhaps the most obvious way in which we can detect this in everyday life is through the great number of words spoken here that come from Náhuatl. Let us consider Popocatepetl and Iztaccihuatl, the two emblematic hills in the Anáhuac valley (the Valley of Mexico), which on clear days can be seen in the distance to the south-east of the city. Despite the best efforts of the Spanish colonists to impose their social structures, language and beliefs, many areas of the city retain their original names: Tlalpan (which means *terra firma*), Iztapalapa (paving stones over water), Coyoacan (the place of the coyote owners), Mixcoac (land of serpents) or Chapultepec (grasshopper hill) are just a few examples. There are other words that are used every day, such as *tlapalería*, which is the word Mexicans use for a hardware shop, deriving from the word *tlap-alli*, which means colour; *itacate*, an afternoon picnic; or *tequio*, which is voluntary work as part of a group. In present day Mexican Spanish, *papalote*, deriving from the Náhuatl word for butterfly, means comet. The word *huey*, which in Náhuatl meant great or venerable, is used nowadays to call out to someone without using their name, and, depending on the tone and context in which it is employed, it can be pejorative, neutral or friendly. It is also said that the various different accents found in Mexico City are influenced by Náhuatl, especially their cadence and melody, and likewise the local custom of searching everywhere for puns, plays on words and risqué double entendres. This practice – known as *albur* – has been studied by linguists and consists of a type of duel based on verbal dexterity. In its typical form someone is considered to have 'won' the exchange when their opponent remains silent or their reply is not as witty.

Many objects of pre-Colombian origin are still used on a daily basis in Mexican households. The most typical are found in the kitchen, where there is almost always a *molcajete* (from the Náhuatl *molcaxtl*, a jar for delicacies), a large mortar – traditionally made from volcanic rock – which is used to grind, prepare

ZÓCALO/TENOCHTITLAN

or serve food, or the *comal* (*comalli*), a griddle traditionally made from baked clay but these days frequently made of metal, on which most Mexicans bake tomatoes and chillies and heat up tortillas. The *metate*, or grindstone, in the form of a small rectangular board which is placed on the floor, is essential for making mole and for grinding maize into flour. Chroniclers such as Fray Bernardino de Sahagún affirm that in ancient Mexico the *metate* was a symbol of femininity, the sound of the stones grinding being associated with women preparing food, as represented in the paintings of Diego Rivera and other 20th-century Mexican artists.

Many people, especially in poorer districts, still sleep on a *petate*, a type of rug or mat woven from a particular type of palm leaf. For the ancient inhabitants of the Anáhuac valley, this object was so highly valued that only the governing caste could sit on the *icpalli*, a throne made of *petates*. These mats also served as the altar on which a bride and groom would receive their blessings. Their use is so widespread that there are numerous idioms in which the word features. For example, to describe a fire that burns fiercely but briefly, or an intense but short-lived passion, we say that it is a *petate* flare. Colloquially, *petatearse* means to die, because the *petate* is also used as a shroud. Other objects of Mexica origin that are quite commonly found are *chiquihuites* (baskets woven from palm leaves that are used to keep tortillas warm) and *tenates* (tall cylindrical baskets in which clothes – or anything else that needs to be stored – are kept). Some of the clothes that the ancient inhabitants of this country wore are still evident today, but in a stylised or adapted form. The most common are *huipiles*, the square-shaped tunics woven using an ancient technique known as back-strap-loom weaving, and it is in these bright clothes (which can be either short or long) that the ancient inhabitants of Anáhauc are depicted in the ancient codices.

*

Mexican cuisine – in which the legacy of ancient Mexico is so apparent – has been declared an intangible heritage of humanity by UNESCO. Some of the basic fruits and vegetables in our cuisine, such as the avocado – known as *aguacate* (*aguacatl*) – or the tomato (*xitomatl*), which are now consumed throughout the world, originated in this land, as did maize, cocoa, chocolate (*xocolatl*) and a large variety of chillies. Eating tortillas is one more ancient custom we inherited, although, according to historians, they were originally thicker than the ones we have today. The process known as nixtamalisation (from the Náhuatl *nixtamalli*) is a very particular way of preparing maize that has survived from the original cultures down through the centuries, enabling vast numbers of people to be fed. The process involves soaking the hard maize kernels in hot water and adding ingredients such as ash, ground sea-shells or chalk to soften and calcify them. After leaving the mixture to rest for a few hours, it is then traditionally ground in a *metate* or in a mill to obtain a soft dough. This process enriches the maize with calcium and other minerals and also increases the bioavailability of the proteins. The dough that has undergone nixtamalisation is used to prepare drinks and dishes, including, among many others, *atole*, tamales and tortillas.

Another gastronomic custom inherited from the ancients is the consumption of *pulque*, an alcoholic drink obtained from the leaves of the agave, which is produced by fermenting the sap, popularly known as *aguamiel*, or honeywater. Because of its density, *pulque* has been used to assuage hunger in times when food has been scarce. This drink is also used as a remedy for gastrointestinal conditions because of the large number of probiotics involved in the fermentation process. *Pulquerías* – establishments in which *pulque* is consumed and with a social function similar to bars or cafés – have always been typical of working-class areas, but they have also become fashionable in recent years with the hipsters who frequent the Roma and Condesa districts. The custom of eating the prickly pear cactus – *Opuntia ficus-indica*, known in Mexico as *nopal* – is also characteristic of the region. This cactus is roasted or eaten cold in a salad mixed with onion and oregano. Owing to its slimy interior and its smooth exterior (once the thorns have been removed) it is not very popular outside the valley or in other regions of the country, but it does have its aficionados.

It is said that when the first inhabitants arrived at Anáhuac food was very scarce, and so they learned to eat the limited fauna that they found there. Iguanas, snakes and armadillos were reserved for the ruling caste, while the ordinary people ate leaves, flowers and insects. Quite a variety of insects are still consumed in Mexico City today, and it is not hard to find them in dishes served in fine-dining restaurants as well as in some regular snack bars. The most common are *chapulines*, a type of grasshopper with a dark or violet colour, which are often served crushed and which have a slightly tart flavour. Not all grasshoppers are eaten, only those of the *Sphenarium* genus. They are collected during a specific season of the year and, once purged, they are roasted on a *comal*. Maguey worms are less common but highly prized. *Escamoles*, which in Náhuatl means ant stew, is also known as Mexican caviar. This dish is prepared with the eggs of *Liometopum apiculatum* ants, who build their nest underground, usually at the base of the maguey plant, in *nopal* fields or next to *pirul* (Peruvian pepper) trees. These black or red ants are extremely aggressive. For that reason, and because it is difficult to maintain production throughout the year, they are very expensive. Like the majority of edible insects, ants contain between 40 and 60 per cent protein, which is why the World Health Organization affirms that, if it became more wide-spread, the practice of eating insects would help protect people across the planet from possible future famines.

*

Unlike Venice, the city of Tenochtitlan was not an archipelago, but it was supported on the lake thanks to a system of agriculture and territorial expansion known as *chinampa* (from the Náhuatl *chinamitl*, meaning 'within a cane fence') that has not completely disappeared. *Chinampas* are large barges constructed on a frame of tree trunks and branches over which organic soil is placed with carefully selected biodegradable elements, such as grass cuttings, leaf mould and the skins of various fruits and vegetables. The technique originated in the era of the Teotihuacana culture (*c.* 2nd–7th centuries CE) but it reached its greatest extent around the year 1519, at which point it covered almost the whole of Lake Xochimilco, located to the south of the city. To provide them with a permanent fixture they are planted with *ahuejote* trees, a type of willow (*Salix bonplandiana*), the roots of which extend down to the lake bed and sometimes even deeper. Combined with other techniques, such as a system of irrigation canals and the construction of *bancales*, or terraces, *chinampas* allowed a very dense population to be supported for centuries. These days only a few survive, but it is possible to find them in the municipalities of Xochimilco and Tláhuac, where groups of farmworkers still cultivate the land as a collective. These are the last traces of an agricultural system that is almost extinct but which it would be very productive to revive.

Despite the fact that it has grown haphazardly, amassing buildings of all styles and types, from the palaces and churches of the Viceroyalty (16th–19th centuries) to the skyscrapers of the 21st century, there are still some pyramids and sacred sites within the boundaries of Mexico City. Located right in the heart of the city, next to the Palacio Nacional (the seat of government) and behind the cathedral, the Templo Mayor (the Huey Teocalli or Great Temple) was the symbolic centre of the enormous tributary network of the Mexica Empire, a place where offerings were made and skull racks known as *tzompantli* were constructed; a place to worship the gods of war and rain; a symbol of the Mexica's triumphs over their enemies. Constructed in honour of the dual divinity (Ometeotl), the twin temples that crown the

pyramid reflect the cosmological vision of a series of opposites – masculine–feminine, heaven–earth, drought–rain, summer solstice–winter solstice – and the cults of the various deities, the principal ones being Tlaloc (the lord of rain and fertility) and Huitzilopochtli, the warrior-god, sun-god and patron of the Mexica. The most import aspects of the empire's political and religious life came together in the Templo Mayor, including sowing ceremonies and the coronations and funerals of the ruling caste (*tlatoanis*). The 1985 earthquake that laid open the heart of Mexico City exposed a large section of this impressive structure. The objects and sculptures discovered there are now on display at the Museo del Templo Mayor, among them the monumental statue of Coyolxauhqui (daughter of the priestess Coatlicue) but also exquisitely delicate shields, spears and earthenware. The main ceremonial centres located in Mexico City are Tlatelolco, Azcapotzalco, Mixcoac and Cuicuilco. Much less well known are the ruins located in the basement of the current Spanish Cultural Centre, possibly the remains of the Calmecac, the school for the children of Tenochtitlan's nobles. It was here that the boys who were destined to become priests, high-ranking warriors, judges, teachers and governors were trained and educated. They were also taught music, astronomy and medicine and they read and memorised the stories illustrated in the codices. The school was a boarding establishment, in which the children lived, ate and slept.

After the Spanish invasion missionary friars played a key role in the process of colonisation. The religious practices of the original cultures were forbidden, under pain of cruel or mortal punishment. In order to facilitate the assimilation of Christianity by the peoples of the Anáhuac valley, the evangelisers took great efforts to fuse the beliefs of two very different cultures into a single religion and a single set of rites and iconography. Many churches in the 16th and 17th centuries were built on sites sacred to the ancient Mexicans. Huitzilopochtli, whom the Mexica associated with the sun, blood and life, was assimilated into the figure of

Christ, while the worship of Coyolxauhqui, associated with the moon, was incorporated into that of the Virgin Mary. Tonantzin, who represented Mother Nature, became identified with the Virgin of Guadalupe (see 'A Woman Clothed with the Sun' on page 61). This allowed practices that the Church considered pagan to be replaced gradually, and, above all, it put a stop to the Indigenous culture being handed down through the generations.

Children are still taught at school that there remain very few traces of what the lives and beliefs of the original peoples were like, and that it is thanks to the letters of the conquistadors or the memoirs of friars such as Bernardino de Sahagún or Toribio de Benavente that we know anything at all about the Náhuatl period. Doubtless the chronicles and books written by these men are interesting and help to give us a good idea of the world that they encountered, but it is important to remember that their interpretation was biased by the influence of their own culture, prejudices and interests. One example of this is the enormous discrepancy between the descriptions of the figure of Huitzilopochtli who, for the chroniclers, was a terrible, insatiable god who demanded human sacrifices but whom the Mexica portrayed as a compassionate, generous warrior who, at the age of twenty-one, led his people on a long journey from the north of Mexico to the valley in which they were finally able to settle. Despite their best intentions, the transcriptions that the friars tried to make of Náhuatl words are at best inaccurate; likewise their descriptions of Indigenous rituals, customs and practices. The study of Mexica culture at universities was carried out on the basis of these biased texts until only a few decades ago, when Mexican historians such as Miguel León-Portilla and Alfredo López Austin began to look for testimonies by the descendants and cultural heirs of the Indigenous peoples. Additionally, from the 16th century onwards, this knowledge was preserved clandestinely and passed down from parent to child and by teacher to pupil right here in Mexico City so that today there are still groups studying *Toltecayotl*. This word

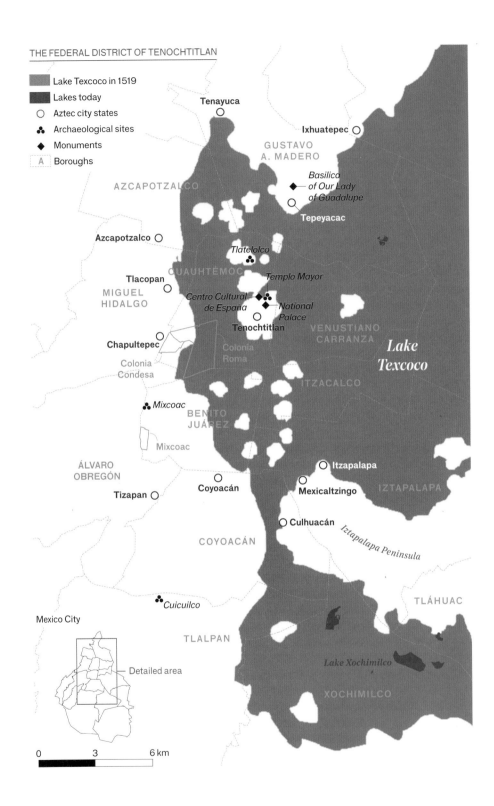

THE FEDERAL DISTRICT OF TENOCHTITLAN

Lake Texcoco in 1519
Lakes today
○ Aztec city states
⚘ Archaeological sites
◆ Monuments
A Boroughs

Tenayuca ○

Ixhuatepec ○

GUSTAVO
A. MADERO

AZCAPOTZALCO

Basilica
◆ of Our Lady
of Guadalupe
○
Tepeyacac

Azcapotzalco ○

Tlatelolco
⚘

CUAUHTÉMOC

Templo Mayor

Tlacopan ○

MIGUEL
HIDALGO

Centro Cultural ◆ ◆⚘
de España ◆ National
○ Palace
Tenochtitlan

Chapultepec ○

VENUSTIANO
CARRANZA

**Lake
Texcoco**

Colonia
Roma

Colonia
Condesa

ITZACALCO

⚘ Mixcoac

BENITO
JUÁREZ

Mixcoac

ÁLVARO
OBREGÓN

○ Itzapalapa

○
Coyoacán

○
Mexicaltzingo

IZTAPALAPA

Tizapan ○

○ Culhuacán

Iztapalapa Peninsula

COYOACÁN

TLÁHUAC

⚘ Cuicuilco

Mexico City

TLALPAN

Lake Xochimilco

Detailed area

XOCHIMILCO

0   3   6 km

was used to refer to the ancient Mexica craftsmen and now, in a contemporary context, to those who study the philosophy and spiritual practices of the Mexica. The aim is to learn, preserve and pass on their ancestors' legacy, including the Náhuatl language as well as their spiritual teachings. According to them, knowledge is not passed on solely through the intellect but also through day-to-day experiences and an empirical learning process. The aim is to develop the enormous potential of human consciousness, and to do this it is important to cultivate willpower. One example of this form of practice is the custom of rising at dawn and taking a bath in freezing-cold water, irrespective of whether one is healthy or sick or what the weather is like. Each of the practices of *Toltecayotl* is taught and supervised by a master, or *temachtiani*. Like Miguel León-Portilla, the followers of this school affirm that the Mexica do not worship gods but rather the forces of nature – such as water, earth, wind and fire – with which we interact on a daily basis. In order to commune with them, they perform ritual dances in which they play sea-shell trumpets, the sound of which opens the four paths, or cardinal points, and perform improvised singing through which each student engages in a search for their innermost self, where their roots connect with everything else.

The anthropologist and historian Ángel María Garibay used to tell his students, 'If you are interested in Mexican antiquity, seek out and get to know a living Indian.' What he meant by this was that the ancient cultures are not dead but survive in the lives of Indigenous people today. Like many a grand metropolis on our planet, Mexico City is made up of migrants from different states and countries. However, what is particular to this city, making it a unique and inimitable place, lies in its Mexica roots, which, consciously or unconsciously, reverberate still in those of us who live here. ✒

Stop that Train

DARÍO ALEMÁN

Translated by Kathryn Phillips-Miles

A group of Central American migrants waits for the goods train to arrive at Tenosique station, Tabasco state, so that they can climb on to the roof and continue their journey northwards. The stretch from Tenosique to Palenque will become part of the route of the Tren Maya.

The Tren Maya is a gift imposed on rather than given to the Indigenous communities of south-eastern Mexico. It is a grandiose and controversial project that President Andrés Manuel López Obrador is determined to see built whatever the cost in order to bring progress to far-flung regions that might just be content with far less.

109

More than a thousand years ago, back in 700 CE, there was a prosperous and powerful kingdom that competed with Tikal and Palenque for dominance over the other Maya peoples of the Yucatán Peninsula. It is said that in its period of greatest splendour it expanded its territory, marking the borders with stakes, all of which were inscribed with the same message: 'Here begins the Kingdom of the Serpent's Head'.

The heart of the kingdom was Calakmul, a city of markets, squares, temples and palaces in the form of pyramids, protected by a warrior caste that was trained from childhood to defend and conquer. It did not need stone walls because it was surrounded by a labyrinth of tropical trees, swamps, rivers and caves that stretched for thousands of square kilometres. There, in the forest, lay its first line of defence, comprised of pumas, jaguars, crocodiles and snakes.

Only a few traces still remain of the impregnable Kingdom of the Serpent's Head. The buildings of its capital are now barely discernible ruins in the undergrowth, where tourists go to be amazed and archaeologists go to work and reconstruct the past. The jungle that once served as a shield is much smaller as a result of so many bites being taken out of it by the cities and towns that sprang up within it. The animals, the wild guardians of Calakmul, just about survive, thanks to being on the International Union for the Conservation of Nature's red list of species at risk of extinction. At the same time, all that remains of the warrior caste, which was subsequently subjected to centuries of genocide and slavery, are a few communities – labelled 'Indigenous' – scattered across what remains of the tropical forest in the centre of Yucatán, impoverished and isolated from 'modern Mexico'.

One of these communities, known as Unión 20 de Junio, is part of the municipality of Calakmul, which, in turn, belongs to the state of Campeche in south-eastern Mexico. However, the locals have never liked this name, and they all prefer to call it La Mancolona.

Surrounded by an impressive mass of trees and sweltering in the humid tropical heat, during the day La Mancolona looks like a ghost town, inhabited only by a few nonchalant dogs. A visitor arriving unannounced might get the impression that everyone had left during night, abandoning their homes and animals. But people do live here – some five hundred according to official statistics – it's just that they don't live their lives on the

DARÍO ALEMÁN is a Cuban journalist based in Mexico City. He reports for the magazine *El Estornudo* and has worked with various independent media organisations in Cuba and internationally.

Central American migrants attempt
to board a moving goods train at
Tenosique station.

community's three small stretches of
semi-asphalted road or on the paths
across the grass that connect the village
huts, but in the *milpas* – cornfields – three
kilometres further into the forest. The
men go there at the crack of dawn to work
the small parcels of land known as *ejidos* –
land that belongs to no one and everyone
at the same time, a type of communal
ownership that was established after
years of war more than a century ago at
the time of the Mexican Revolution. The
members of the community grow food for
their families here and collect honey on a
commercial scale, and they do not return
home until after nightfall. In the meantime, the women spend the day at the back
of their huts stripping maize in disciplined

silence, cooking in rustic stone ovens or
looking after the children, chickens and
goats.

This is all explained by Sebastián
Moreno Jiménez, and he later reveals that,
despite everything, they have a good life
here – it could be better, but at least they
have their own land. A small, slim twenty-
year-old, Sebastián is a descendant of the
ancient Maya of Calakmul, the warrior
people of the Kingdom of the Serpent's
Head, and, like them, he was born in the
jungle.

Sebastián returned in early 2022, two
years after leaving for good – or so he'd
thought at the time. When he reappeared
everyone was too busy working to notice,
but later, when they saw him, they were
all astonished. No one who had had the
chance to go away and study at university had ever set foot back in this remote
corner of Mexico where there are no

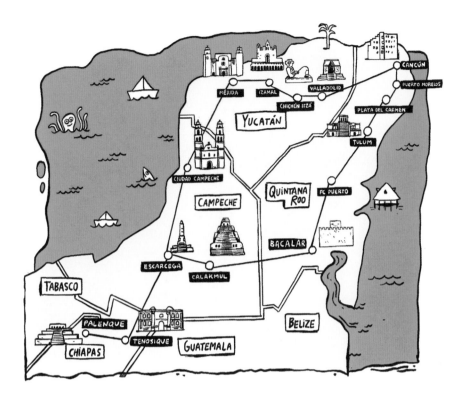

mobile phones, no hospitals and no supermarkets and where the only job to be had is working in the *milpas*, growing crops and looking after bees. 'They didn't understand why I'd come back. They thought it had all gone wrong for me in the city and that I'd got into trouble. But it wasn't that. I came back because this is where I'm from, and I want to fight against the Tren Maya, and I'm able to do that,' he says with a smile.

It was his family who had encouraged him to go and study at Hopelchén, a small city located around a hundred kilometres to the north, also in the state of Campeche. He started a bachelor's degree in administration, but after a few months he switched to industrial engineering. For two years he combined his studies with work in order to pay for his accommodation. He never complained or asked for

any help. He wanted to make his community proud of him, become successful and learn more about the world than any of his forebears, who had rarely left the borders of the Yucatán Peninsula and had never, ever, crossed the sea.

Hopelchén was a good place to begin his journey towards success. While not a big city, it has shops, squares, parks, a university, hospitals and places set aside for leisure, things that don't exist in his community. However, in spite of its charms, people in cities do not live on the land like they do in La Mancolona, nor do people know each other like they are all members of the same family nor do they speak to each other in Tzeltal or Ch'ol, the two languages that were spoken in these parts long before the Europeans introduced Castilian at the point of a sword. He was amazed by the modernity and

> 'The project in question is the Tren Maya: a metallic anaconda that will run for 1,500 kilometres around the Yucatán Peninsula, like a snake biting its own tail. They say that once it is up and running progress will follow.'

progress but not seduced by them, at least not enough to stop him from going back home as soon as he learned that several Indigenous communities in the Yucatán, his own included, had joined together to stop the most ambitious project to be promoted by President Andrés Manuel López Obrador.

*

The project in question is the Tren Maya: a metallic anaconda that will run for 1,500 kilometres around the Yucatán Peninsula, like a snake biting its own tail. It will run through cities, towns, ancient ruins and dense forests full of wildlife, throughout the five states of south-east Mexico (Tabasco, Chiapas, Quintana Roo, Yucatán and Campeche) at great speed, again and again, its belly swollen with workers, tourists and merchandise. They say that once it is up and running progress will follow in its wake.

This project, which is highly ambitious and costly, emerged from López Obrador's precocious pharaonic fantasies when he became president of Mexico in 2018. Supposedly the Tren Maya, which he himself christened, will be his legacy, the imposing construction by which he will be remembered for decades to come, his tangible imprint on history. That is why he insists that it should be ready by December 2023, six months prior to him leaving office, and that is why he is increasingly quick to pounce on any detractors, who range from ecological movements (or 'pseudo-environmentalists' as he calls them) to his traditional opponents from other parties. One way or another, the Tren Maya will be the door through which he departs when he leaves power, and for that reason it appears he will stop at nothing.

It is of no consequence that the political opposition, the press, human rights organisations and intellectual and academic groups across Mexico all criticise him for building a train that threatens to destroy the natural and archaeological treasures of the Maya Forest or for handing over management of the project's construction to the army, which is one of the country's most opaque and corrupt institutions. López Obrador goes on the attack every morning in his televised speeches, accusing the 'neoliberal elites' and '*fifís*' (the culturally and economically privileged) of being the historical antagonists of the true Mexican people, who, he claims, are naturally humble and virtuous.

For their part, the poor see him as their champion against the oligarchy and could even be said to adore him, affectionately dubbing him *el viejito*, 'the little old man', and declaring that in the next elections they will vote for whoever he designates as his successor, male or female. The poor, who are in the majority in the south-east, have also welcomed news of the train with open arms, as they usually do with any of the president's initiatives. They have their reasons. No other leader has created as many social programmes as he has, or increased the non-contributory old-age pension as much, or offered bi-monthly financial support to people with disabilities. And although these subsidies are for very modest amounts they make a huge difference in the less developed areas of Mexico.

There is an old proverb that says that if you want to feed a man for a day you can offer him a fish, but if you want him always to have food you should give him a fishing rod and teach him how to fish. In the south-east, this story has become interwoven in the popular imagination with the Tren Maya, which has become the fishing rod and López Obrador the good citizen who provides it. The president affirms that his project is going to 'put a rocket under sustainable development' in the region, that the carriages will be crammed with investors as well as tourists ready to spend their dollars and euros here so they can discover the hidden wonders of the forest, that prosperous cities will spring up around every station, that there will be no more unemployment and that all this will happen in a sort of domino effect. Although the contagious enthusiasm created by his words has grown at a much faster rate than the construction works – partly because as soon as they clear the ground to lay the rails they discover thousands of archaeological objects and areas of archaeological interest – many people are already saying that they can feel the first hints of the promised modernity. A new aqueduct to supply water to the planned stations, an asphalted road for lorries to distribute goods. Everything here is treated as if it were a direct consequence of the Tren Maya, and it is celebrated and appreciated.

*

No one in La Mancolona can remember a drought lasting as long as the one in 2019. The forest's leafy vegetation has always attracted continuous, heavy downpours; however, for the first time in a long while the sky remained cloudless for four months at the height of the rainy season.

Sebastián's recollections of those days are focused on his uncle, Nicolás Moreno. Nicolás, a sturdy, hard-working man, well respected in several Indigenous communities in Campeche for his proud demeanour and air of leadership, was clearly very worried at that time. More than that, he was downright sad. He would come back from the *milpa*, slump into a chair and tell the same story every day – how the soil was harder than yesterday, how the crops were being lost and the bees had fewer flowers from which to gather nectar. Things were no better in his house, just like all the other houses in La Mancolona. At that time their water supply came through a system of pipes thirty kilometres long, drawing from the river in the village of Bel-ha, but the pump that drove the system had broken down just as it had stopped raining. There was nothing that the members of the community could do except wait for the tropical showers and collect what they could in plastic receptacles, just as their ancestors had hundreds of years ago using large terracotta jars.

That was a terrible year, but no one in La Mancolona could imagine that the following year would be even worse and that a pandemic would decimate the community and other villages in the state. By the end of November, however, many people thought that 2020 would see the start of a bonanza, a hope that was reinforced when a handful of local officials from Morena, the president's party, deigned to make an appearance in those parts. The officials requested a meeting with all the residents. They said that they wanted to consult them on how two of the social programmes promoted by the government were panning out: Sembrando Vida (which means Sowing Life) and Jóvenes Construyendo el Futuro (Young People Building the Future). Since the creation of Sembrando Vida, López Obrador has guaranteed state incentives for agricultural production and small-scale reforestation in places like La Mancolona, while the Jóvenes Construyendo el Futuro programme has reduced unemployment rates among men and women between the ages of eighteen and twenty-nine who live in the country's poorest areas. That is why many people in the community thought that the 'little old man' must be some kind of saint. No politician, at least as far as the oldest members of the community could remember, had ever shown any interest in social programmes that had genuine impact on their lives.

According to Sebastián, Nicolás made a particularly strong impression at that meeting. When it was his turn to speak, he began by saying the collection system had led to commercial structures that were unfair on La Mancolona's honey producers. The honey produced in the community could only be sold to a couple of firms, who bought it at very low prices, put it in jars, stuck on a grandiose label extolling its exclusive, 100 per cent organic production and sold it at exorbitant prices in Mexico's big cities and even abroad. There was also little point in allocating funds to eradicate youth unemployment when communities like theirs did not have the necessary infrastructure to guarantee a minimum standard of education, or when the teachers, who lived in other villages, could barely find transport to reach the school, or when the only work opportunities offered in La Mancolona were to strip maize, look after the farm animals and work in the *milpas*.

BY POPULAR DEMAND

The Calakmul Biosphere, designated a natural reserve since 1989, is home to 80 per cent of the Yucatán Peninsula's plant species, 350 species of bird and almost a hundred different mammals. The jungle has a particularly high concentration of jaguars, the big cats worshipped by the Maya that once roamed the Americas from Maryland to the southern tip of South America. Now, as a result of hunting, deforestation and urban expansion, they are found in less than half of that territory, and their population has been in long-term decline. In recent years, however, the International Union for the Conservation of Nature (IUCN) and other NGOs have been working to save the Yucatán's jungles, and the protection of jaguars is central to these projects – as an 'umbrella species', protecting them has a cascading positive effect in their habitat. Much of the work of the Jaguar Alliance involves the locals, setting up agreements between the government and agricultural communities in Calakmul, who are transitioning from keeping livestock and practising illegal deforestation to forest stewardship and the cultivation of products such as melipona honey and chicle from the chicozapote tree, which is used to make a sustainable chewing gum. The jaguar population increased from 4,025 in 2010 to 4,766 in 2018 as a consequence. Once the news had spread, the government agreed it would plan the route of the Tren Maya with conservation requirements in mind, provisionally agreeing to expand the Calakmul reserve and link it to others in the area. If it keeps its word, Mexico will have one of the world's largest protected areas.

Clockwise from above: Laundry, Maya ruins and tourists in Palenque, one of Mexico's most important archaeological sites but also one of its poorest areas; it has been promised that the construction of the Tren Maya will bring prosperity to the region.

'Everyone gave him a round of applause, and the visiting gentlemen tried to calm them down, promising solutions. Afterwards they asked people to sign a document which, they said, was to show whether we were in favour of the social programmes. Of course, although the programmes were not problem free, we all signed. A short while later the Xpujil Indigenous People's Regional Council, known as CRIPX [Consejo Regional Indígena y Popular de Xpujil], summoned all the communities in the Calakmul municipality to a meeting to discuss the Tren Maya,' relates Sebastián, who by that time had just left for Hopelchén.

THE PASSENGER   Darío Alemán

'Indigenous democracy is based on a very simple principle: everyone's voice is equal.'

Over the centuries numerous books have been written that attempt to define democracy, countless wars have been waged in its name and people have searched high and low, in ancient Greece and revolutionary utopias, and still no one seems totally happy. No one has come here to look at CRIPX or any of the places where the Indigenous communities meet to create solutions for their collective problems, where people are not even clear what democracy is, and that doesn't worry them. CRIPX is the nearest thing to a parliamentary government that can be imagined, although in reality it is only a community organisation. Its meetings are open; in other words, anyone – whether young, old, illiterate, farmers, bee-keepers, men or women – can participate, sit down on one of the benches in the old courtyard where it meets, raise their hand when they agree and debate in Spanish, Tzeltal or in another Maya language. Indigenous democracy is a demonstrable fact that does not need a highly educated 'indigenist' to explain it, because it is based on a very simple principle: everyone's voice is equal.

The headquarters of CRIPX is in the village of Xpujil, a very poor place that depends for its livelihood on the handful of backpackers who camp there overnight before visiting the nearby Maya ruins at Calakmul. Federal Highway 186 passes through the village as it runs from one end of the Yucatán Peninsula to the other, connecting towns and villages in Campeche to those in Quintana Roo. The numerous cars and lorries travelling along this road rarely make a stop here.

The road is the only thing that connects Xpujil with the rest of the world, and it is also a kind of torment of Tantalus for the villagers, who are desperate for progress. This progress, they say, will finally arrive with the Tren Maya, which will locate one of its eighteen stations there. In the meantime the village gets by with its asphalted streets, its inns, its markets selling clothes *Made in China* and its tiny medical centre, which is much more than you will find forty-three kilometres deeper into the forest in La Mancolona.

At the CRIPX meeting Nicolás and several of his neighbours learned that the papers they had signed were actually a statement of support for the Tren Maya, part of a show of transparency on the part of López Obrador's government to demonstrate that the vast majority (92 per cent) of Indigenous people who live in the forest through which the train will pass had given their permission for this to happen. This was not the government's only sleight of hand. In some communities the officials spoke about the benefits of the megaproject and refused to answer any questions about its potential environmental and social impact, or they hid the fact that the construction of the stretch of track to Calakmul would require the felling of 283 hectares of tropical forest, the equivalent of more than four hundred football pitches. In other communities they didn't translate from Spanish, or only translated selectively, the reasons behind the consultation process, and in others they faked the signatures of individuals who had never been consulted. Among those attending the meeting, some believed that the Tren Maya would lead to deforestation and the destruction of the peninsula's *cenotes* (underground caverns and caves that hold the country's largest reserves of fresh water), and others thought that, with a bit of luck, the president's initiative would bring prosperity to their villages. However, all of them felt that they had been duped and betrayed.

The promise of modernity that would accompany the train, even if it were true, wouldn't ever be realised; they no longer wanted it.

*

Since the first human beings arrived here many thousands of years ago, the history of the Yucatán has been a constant fight between modernity and tradition, a bloody clash of different worldviews, a cyclical confrontation between those who claim to be the standard-bearers of progress and those who carry the stigma of barbarism. The history of the Yucatán, at the end of the day, is the same as that of any other scrap of land in Latin America.

It was the same when the Maya chose to settle in this area and in no time at all established impressive city states that traded with each other and shared the same religion, later expanding towards the south as far as the areas we now call Honduras and El Salvador, subjugating smaller communities and forcing them to accept their system of kings and castes and to worship their gods in sacred temples that they raised above the lush forest, where the priests made human sacrifices and studied mathematics, medicine and astronomy. And it was also the same – even more so – when waves of adventurers arrived from Europe to claim these lands in the name of their monarchs and, incidentally, make off with gold, noble titles and slaves at the expense of the original

STATE-OPERATED TOURISM

Tourism in Mexico, which generates more than 8 per cent of GDP, has always been a business driven by the state. A whole century before the Tren Maya the Mexican government 'invented' Acapulco, an experiment that was repeated in the 1970s when the government employed computer modelling and the country's best brains to select the site for a new tourist city, choosing a fifteen-kilometre strip of jungle off the coast of Quintana Roo, Cancún – a story told in Robert J. Dunphy's entertaining 1972 *New York Times* article ('Why the Computer Chose Cancún'). Half a century later Cancún's airport attracts more international flights than any other Mexican city. The success of the initiative showed that tourism – *la industria sin chimeneas* (the industry without chimneys), as it was called – could bring development to rural areas, and over the following decades inspired similar operations along the Caribbean coast, which was rebranded the Riviera Maya in the 2000s. The next stop for development is Bacalar, forty kilometres from the border with Belize, one of the new railway stations on the Tren Maya line. Bacalar's main attraction is a freshwater lagoon that the tourist brochures refer to as the 'lagoon of seven colours' after the different shades the water – fed by underground *cenotes* and particularly pure – turns, depending on the light. In 2020, after a storm, the lagoon turned brown and stayed brown for six months, highlighting how difficult it can be to build a tourist industry – even without chimneys – around a natural wonder without destroying it.

Family members outside their house near what will be a section of the Tren Maya line between Palenque and Tenosique.

inhabitants, who at that time were experiencing a collapse of what had once been their powerful civilisation.

One of the first encounters between the Maya and these fortune hunters took place when they discovered a shipwreck on their coast. The only two survivors were taken as slaves, but they obtained their freedom shortly afterwards. One of them left in search of an outpost of Spanish conquistadors; the other, in contrast, decided to stay with his former captors. His name was Gonzalo Guerrero. He adopted native clothing, learned their languages and worshipped their gods. He tied back his hair and tattooed his body like them, had his ears, nose and lips pierced with obsidian and maguey thorns, married and had a daughter. In many villages in the Yucatán he was accepted as a respected military chieftain. He's known today as the 'father of the mestizos', a title which might be rather too optimistic, created in order to disguise the historic reality of Mexico and promote the story that the nation's formation was a harmonious process based on ethnic diversity and multiculturalism. In fact, Guerrero's was an isolated case and not at all representative of what the conquest and so-called 'mixing of the races' entailed. His exceptional status is explained by his death: he was killed by an arrow through the chest as he fought against his former comrades, who considered him a traitor and a heretic if not an outright lunatic, and also by the following twenty years of war, during which the Spaniards imposed their language, their God and their Latin masses by fire and sword, built their own cities and abandoned the monumental Maya temples and palaces to the dense forest, consigning them to oblivion.

Three centuries later the Creoles (a mixed race of conquerors and the conquered, people who boasted of their European blood but rejected that of their Indigenous ancestors, who were the first people to call themselves Mexicans) expelled the Spaniards, founded the nation and declared themselves lords of all that was enclosed within its borders. However, the spirit of the conquest persisted in these pettifogging, warmongering patriarchs who abolished slavery on paper but in reality retained it for those who were not mestizo and those who were not quite white enough to be truly free. For the Maya, independence, the 'patriotic wars' and republican ideas were in large part irrelevant and just meant the exchange of one exploiter for another, a transfer of their vassalage. That was why, in 1848, the Indigenous peoples of the Yucatán Peninsula unleashed their fury against their new masters, a fury expressed with their machetes with which, over the course of eight years, they killed 250,000 rich white men, who were by then arguing among themselves over whether or not to make the Yucatán an independent republic separate from Mexico. The Maya rebellion, known as the Caste War of Yucatán, ended in 1901, drowned in blood by the federal army in the name of national integrity. Those who survived fled into the deep forest, where they re-established their communities.

The descendants of the twice-vanquished Maya are still there, in the same forest where their ancestors lived. Today they are citizens who can vote. Today the law gives them the same rights as other Mexicans. However, today they are also the country's poorest citizens. The modern history of Mexico, tainted with corruption and violence, has forgotten about the south-east, a region where in four of the five states the average household income is much lower than the national average, and where 7.3 million people are living in poverty, of which 2.2 million are in a condition of extreme poverty.

Modernity in these places is just an illusion, as well as serving as the excuse perpetually available to some of the people (the modernisers) to subjugate the others (the barbarians). After so many centuries progress has yet to settle in this region. While it is fair to say that it has always gravitated there, it has never managed to stick, to find a form. However, progress has a historical legacy that the Maya of Yucatán can readily notice in the gradual disappearance of their ancient languages, in their poverty, in the indiscriminate invasion of the beaches by luxury hotels and in the shrinking of the Calakmul tropical forest, which is the second largest biosphere reserve on the continent.

*

When Sebastián is not at home you can find him in the Centro Comunitario de Aprendizaje, the Community Learning Centre (CCA), one of few concrete buildings in La Mancolona and the only place for miles around with access to the internet, thanks to a small satellite dish on its roof. He has been able to continue his studies from there – online – as well as teach his neighbours how to use a computer, search the internet and communicate on Facebook. Now, he says, he is going to offer a fairly basic mathematics course in Spanish and Tzeltal, which anyone can attend, regardless of age. And he could do more, a lot more, if it were not for the fact only three of the CCA's fourteen computers (obtained thanks to CRIPX and grants from various NGOs) are still working, or if the community had enough money to repair or replace them.

Also, for the past few months he has been responsible for CRIPX's public relations, focusing on social media, providing information about the council's community events, statements and other initiatives. His work as an activist, in common with that of his colleagues, has not been at all easy and has at times seemed to be grinding to a halt. Until shortly after his return, CRIPX was celebrating its success in the lawsuit that it had brought against the government. After long and convoluted legal procedures the community organisation had convinced a judge to order a halt to the construction in Calakmul. But, in violation of this injunction, the excavators returned to the forest, this time with a military escort. According to López Obrador, handing the management of the Tren Maya to the army is a kind of insurance against future privatisation of the project – but it also flies in the face of popular protest. With every day that passes it becomes more difficult to recruit people to the struggle against the train. The frequent patrols of men in camouflage jackets carrying high-calibre weapons, riding in pickup trucks up and down the region's highways put a stop to numerous initiatives. Other people, according to Sebastián, choose not to demonstrate out of fear that one fine day the 'little old man', tired of his detractors, might punish the Indigenous communities of the Yucatán by withdrawing the funding for social programmes. While both of these threats – that of gunshots and the withdrawal of money – might be relatively unlikely, the fear is understandable, all the more so because 'not having

A DANGEROUS PROFESSION

With sixty-one journalists and media workers murdered between 2016 and 2020 and nineteen in 2022 (UNESCO figures), Mexico continues to top the list of the most dangerous countries to work in as a reporter. As well as the killings, Mexican journalists are threatened, kidnapped and tortured, and, in most cases, those responsible for the threats and attacks are public officials or members of the state security forces (local police and various branches of the armed forces). But there is also no shortage of attacks orchestrated by the many criminal groups operating in the country, who are often organised as paramilitaries. Covering the tangled webs of corruption and violence that characterise the relationship between political power, business and organised crime is the highest-risk activity for journalists, but the precariousness and exploitation brought about by the media operators themselves also help to make them extremely vulnerable. Average pay is pitiful, and the labour market has gradually moved towards work with no kind of employment protection, and most of the journalists killed in Mexico in recent years belonged to this most vulnerable and exploited section of the profession. To the numbers of journalists targeted we can also add activists and defenders of human and environmental rights, who work tirelessly in Mexico to challenge the indiscriminate exploitation of energy and mineral resources and against the abuses that often accompany the construction of megaprojects. In 2021 fifty-four environmentalists were killed in Mexico out of a total of 157 across the whole of Latin America (source: Global Witness). (F.M.)

An abandoned wagon from an old train on a stretch of line that will be brought back into use when the Tren Maya is constructed.

much to lose' means that if you do lose you might lose everything.

Sebastián knows – of course he does – that the train will bring progress. Possibly not for his community and possibly not for any of the others in the Yucatán, at least not directly. But there will be work, both for him when he finally graduates and also for other young Maya who have not been able to study at university but who will surely find jobs as gardeners or caretakers in the tourist resorts that will spring up across the peninsula when the train starts running.

Sebastián knows – of course he does – that progress in itself is not a problem but that it becomes a problem when it happens in the wrong place and when it is imposed from on high, and that sometimes all that is needed is a question in order to stop it happening. The question would not be 'Do you or don't you want the Tren Maya?' but rather 'What do you want?' If they had asked the second question, he says, he would have asked for a pump so that his neighbours could have water again, and mobile phones and internet masts, and a fair system of trading so that his uncle could make a living from the honey he collects and his aunt could sell the handi-crafts that she spends her mornings making from orange skins and toucan feathers, and, if it is not too much to ask, a medical centre with basic equipment so that the sick do not die on the way to hospitals in far-flung cities.

Progress in La Mancolona, the type that they want in La Mancolona, is much less expensive than a train. 🐦

ELENA REINA

Translated by Kathryn Phillips-Miles

Elena Perez from Nicaragua travelling to
Mexico in search of her daughter Carla,
who disappeared seventeen years ago in
Ciudad Juárez on her way to the USA.

A Girl All Alone by the Side of the Road

The death of nineteen-year-old Debanhi Escobar provoked extraordinary levels of media attention, turning a spotlight on the tragedy of femicides in Mexico, the scourge of a rotten judicial system and the impunity enjoyed by the killers. Above all, it lit a fire under a feminist movement that has become a thorn in the government's side.

L ook at her, over there all alone. With her black skirt and white top, her hands hugging her body, her hair wafting over her shoulders every time a lorry speeds past along the dark road. She has just got out of a taxi in the middle of nowhere. Who knows why, although any woman could guess. Just as any woman could feel the cold sweat that sends shivers down her spine, her heart in her mouth, her brain working much faster than her legs, the primal awareness of being held captive by someone stronger than her, as if she can smell it. She starts running. She's by the side of the road. She goes into a motel, the only place with lights on in this industrial estate in the north-east of Mexico. She looks into a closed restaurant. She's lost. She's face down. Floating lifelessly in a tank of dirty water.

Her name was Debanhi Escobar, and she was nineteen years old. Her body was there for twelve days, decomposing at the same rate as the institution charged with the responsibility of finding her.

No woman in Mexico, a country where eleven women are viciously murdered every day, will ever be able to forget that image. A girl all alone by the side of the road, at the key moment that will determine her fate, the final hours of her life. There are thousands of Debanhis. The nightmare of any mother, father, brother or sister every time they go out and do what any nineteen-year-old girl would do, what any young girl deserves to be able to do without the fear of never returning home.

That night, 9 April 2002, Debanhi had gone out in Monterrey, Nuevo Léon, the city in which she lived, the second richest city in the country. It is a prosperous and conservative area of Mexico that looks more towards Texas than to the poor Indigenous south that it frequently disowns. Those who run the state – young, white, good looking, wealthy – promised to put so much space between their state and the problems in the rest of the country that they forgot that Nuevo León was still part of Mexico. Only one of them – the governor, Samuel García – had actually been elected to office; the other is his wife, the influencer Mariana Rodríguez, whose job it is to raise the couple's profile through Instagram and TikTok. As if the fake proximity of social media means really knowing what is going on in the streets.

ELENA REINA is a journalist at the Spanish daily *El País*, prior to which she worked for eight years in the newsroom of the Mexican edition of *El País*, where she covered drug trafficking, migration and femicide. In 2020 she won a Gabriel García Márquez Journalism Award. She is co-author of the book *Rabia: crónicas contra el cinismo en América Latina* (Anagrama, 2022).

'Debanhi was not the first woman to disappear in this city that year, and she wouldn't be the last, but her case became a symbol for the disappearance and murder of thousands of women all over Mexico.'

And that particular night the inhospitable road in Monterrey was revealed to them and to the whole country as just one more road that could be in any other city where girls disappear. And if there's no body, there's no crime. And the women who disappear with no one apart from their families searching for them have to be added to those eleven women who are murdered every day, and, in an instant, eleven every day becomes too small a number.

Debanhi was not the first woman to disappear in this city that year, and she wouldn't be the last, but her case became a symbol for the disappearance and murder of thousands of women all over the country. Twelve days of suffering that heightened feelings of rage and impotence, knowing that once more, after grieving for her, nothing would happen.

Debanhi disappeared that night in April, just as María Fernanda Contreras had a few days earlier and many others would during the first three months of the year. The state of Nuevo León was at boiling point. Feminist protest marches against the disappearance of women reached the doors of the governor's office. Collective psychosis was unleashed, particularly among the wealthy, although it was already present among the poorer sections of the population. And Samuel García and Mariana Rodríguez desperately latched on to Debanhi's story – but not to any other – as a burning issue in

order to save their administration, which had fallen short in the same way as every other. Because neither this government nor any previous government had ever bothered to get to grips with the reasons that lie behind the fact that fewer than 10 per cent of gender-based crimes of violence are ever solved.

Posters of Debanhi by the side of the road, her hair wafting in the breeze, were pasted up in cities and neighbourhoods both in Nuevo León and elsewhere. Samuel and Mariana made direct announcements through their social media accounts so that everyone was aware that they had begun a tireless search. Groups representing 'the disappeared' from neighbouring states also joined in the hunt. The story was covered live by every TV channel in the country, and two weeks later something was revealed that the TV executives had not expected to uncover: the failings of a rotten legal system incapable of carrying out a serious investigation. The case fell apart in the hands of anyone who touched it, while the young girl was decomposing in the water tank.

On at least four occasions they had combed the area, organised search parties, had searched the motel where she went early that morning. Nothing. Until twelve days later the young girl's body was found right there, exactly where they had thoroughly and inexpertly searched. But too many days had gone by, and valuable time had been lost, greatly reducing the

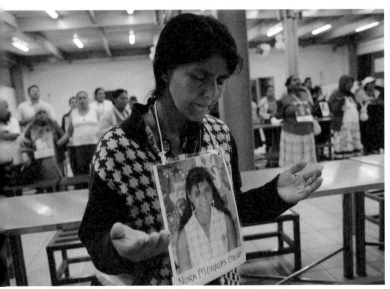

Top to bottom: Suyapa Muñoz, from Honduras, walks the streets of Tequisquiapan with a portrait of her daughter Diana Maribel, who disappeared seventeen years ago in Mexico; Lidia Morales, from Guatemala, prays during a mass at the migrant reception centre in San Luis Potosí; Maria Eugenia Barrera, a Nicaraguan mother, with a photo of her daughter Clementina del Carmen, who disappeared nine years ago.

On 7 September 2021 the Supreme Court of Justice of the Nation ruled that the penalisation of abortion in Mexico is unconstitutional. This means that the court now requires every judge in the country, both federal and local, to deem rules criminalising abortion unconstitutional across all thirty-two states that make up the federation. But each of the individual states must reform its own penal code if women are to stop being imprisoned for crimes relating to abortion. In 2010 the state of Guanajuato, one of the most conservative and Catholic in Mexico, found itself in the media spotlight because its jails were full of women sentenced to more than thirty years' imprisonment for having miscarried. They were often accused of homicide with the kinship of mother and foetus as an aggravating factor. Many of them were illiterate and/or Indigenous, did not even know what crime they had been accused of and had not had access to adequate defence counsel. It took years for them to be freed after a persistent media campaign. Since 2021 it has been legal in Mexico to have an abortion up to twelve weeks after conception, but in practice there are significant differences between states, and in 2022 there were almost a thousand cases of criminal charges being brought for abortion in the states of Tamaulipas, Mexico City, Nuevo León, Mexico and Baja California linked to technicalities in local legislation. (F.M.)

chances of finding out what had happened that night.

Before she was found at the motel, her disappearance had already turned into a macabre show. Debanhi had gone out partying. She had got out of the taxi a few metres from the motel. The taxi driver had taken that photo of her all alone by the side of the road. She had not returned home. Her father had missed calls from her in the early hours of the morning. The taxi driver was the first and only suspect; there would be no other. Her father turned out not to be her biological father. 'Why didn't you answer the phone?' he was asked with disingenuous curiosity by presenters from a local TV channel. The friends who went out with her that night weren't really her friends either, and they traipsed from one TV studio the next to speculate on her whereabouts. She had been drunk. After she was found, one presenter suggested she could have had drugs in her handbag. The show went on.

Throughout those days, when people were confused and worried that she would never be found (in Mexico this would be worse than being worried about finding her dead), the tiniest detail would appear in the national press. Debanhi's father, Mario Escobar, became the spokesman for thousands of parents all over the country who were searching for their children.

9 April, early morning. Mario Escobar receives a message at six o'clock in the morning from his daughter's friends with the photograph of the young girl. The picture that no one can subsequently get out of their heads. They identify the spot: kilometre 15.5 on the road from Monterrey to Nuevo Laredo. The Nueva Castilla Motel is opposite, where her phone was connected for the last time. That's when Debanhi's parents call the missing-persons' helpline, Locatel, the hospitals

> '**But Guerrero made a big mistake. Mexico might still be Mexico, but Mexican women were no longer the same. His explanation angered the feminist movement, which was now stronger than ever.**'

and the coroner's office. They make an official submission about a missing person at the Public Prosecutor's Office and request images from the public CCTV cameras that monitor the city and its entry points. That day the authorities issue a notice with a photograph of her face.

10 April. To avoid the climate of tension that occurred around the cases of other missing girls, the governor sets in motion an emergency search for Debanhi. Usually a search is initiated after seventy-two hours, enough time for nobody ever to be found.

11 April. The operation gets up and running. It is the first ever large deployment of police officers to search for a young girl. More than two hundred police comb the area.

One day later Debanhi's family organises a search that begins near the Nueva Castilla Motel. A base is set up there made up of family members, friends and search parties from other Mexican states, notably mothers who have become experts in excavating the soil and distinguishing an animal bone from a human bone just by looking at it.

On 15 April the Local Search Commission offers a reward of 100,000 pesos (almost $5,000) to whoever can provide any clue as to her whereabouts. One day later, 16 April, the State of Nuevo León General Public Prosecutor's Office makes requests to the authorities of all the states for their help in finding Debanhi. The same office advises that in states such as Tamaulipas, Durango and Baja California,

a number of actions have been undertaken relating to the case, but, to date, the results have been negative.

17 April. She will be found soon, but no one knows this yet. Her parents, family members and friends continue the search. They comb the area where the young girl was last seen and photographed. Her family and friends are accompanied by officers from the Fuerza Civil (State Police Force) and feminist groups. They set out from the motel. Mario Escobar tells people that the Nuevo León Public Prosecutor's Office has shown him fifteen videos that could help the investigation. They will never be of any use. But the entire state apparatus was doing its duty by simulating a historic search.

On 19 April a search for personal effects belonging to Debanhi is undertaken by the Nuevo León Public Prosecutor's Office Specialising in Missing Persons at a condominium in a residential block in the centre of the state capital, Monterrey. Nothing is found.

21 April. The head of the National Search Commission, Karla Quintana, travels to the state of Nuevo León and meets Debanhi's parents to update them on the investigation.

Almost two weeks after the young girl disappeared the alarm is raised when two members of staff at the Nueva Castilla Motel reported a 'foul smell' coming from a disused water tank.

22 April, Friday. Debanhi's father confirms that his daughter's body has

been found inside an abandoned water tank at the Nueva Castilla Motel, just a few metres from the spot where she was last seen. Just a few metres from where everyone gathered to begin the search, the exact spot where her phone had last been connected. In the same place where four searches had been undertaken. Mario Escobar's furious declaration at the entrance to the motel echoed throughout the whole country: 'Thirteen days, and she was here all the time! How many times did they search here?'

After all this one might think that those in charge would have toppled like ninepins. That the governor, at the very least, would be so wounded that it would be difficult to repair his image let alone allow him to stand as a candidate for the presidency in 2024. That when the young girl's body was found floating face down in the water tank, in the exact spot where so many searches had been ineptly carried out, the state would have had a robust response. That the search for the truth about what actually happened that night, without permitting any more errors, would begin right then. Someone who knows very little about Mexico might think all this, and they would be right to do so. However, that is not what happened. Quite the opposite.

THE STUTTERING LEGAL SYSTEM
It can't happen that often that so much awkwardness and so many pallid, sweaty faces have been seen at a press conference. The first important official communication about the case of the year was given by a man who looked as if he'd just seen a corpse – and that corpse was none other than his own. His grave had been dug, his coffin prepared, he was about to be embalmed and there were only a few months left before he would inevitably

topple. This was Gustavo Adolfo Guerrero, the general public prosecutor of Nuevo León, a man not used to having to give explanations to anyone other than his boss, the governor. But that afternoon all the attention was on him. This would be the first day of the end of his career.

If anyone thought that the state Public Prosecutor's Office had hit rock bottom with the search for Debanhi, they were mistaken. There was still further to fall. Finding Debanhi's body at the motel was just the beginning of a whole chain of errors that made the whole of Mexico feel embarrassed by an institution which, up until that point, had managed to get off scot-free despite making so many mistakes.

That afternoon the public prosecutor, appearing with the victim's father and the coroner who had signed the first autopsy, claimed that the young girl had died as a result of a 'sharp blow to her head'. From the platform he suggested that the girl could have fallen into the water tank by herself. As often happens in cases of gender-based violence, he sowed seeds of doubt about a fatal mistake made by the young girl. It might have been her fault. He stuttered and stammered in response to the journalists' questions. There was no evidence for his suspicions. Only the certainty that if she had fallen, perhaps the Public Prosecutor's Office would have some chance of repairing its image.

But Guerrero made a big mistake. Mexico might still be Mexico, but Mexican women were no longer the same. His explanation angered the feminist movement, which was now stronger than ever. The only real opposition to take to the streets against Andrés Manuel López Obrador's government were the thousands of young girls all over the country who began setting monuments on fire,

On 7 March 2020 Mexico woke up to an unusual situation, with schools, workplaces and public institutions staffed almost exclusively by men. Women of all ages had taken part in the strike (billed as #UnDíaSinNosotras, 'a day without us') called for the day before International Women's Day to protest against the rise in cases of femicide. Women's voices have been growing louder in Mexico in recent years, and some concrete results have also been achieved, such as the decriminalisation of abortion (see 'Legislation on Paper' on page 129) and the inclusion of gender quotas in many settings. At the elections in Tlaxcala, however, some individuals tried to get around quotas; because the men's quotas had already been filled, eighteen candidates presented as self-identified transgender women. Also in the 2021 elections, this time in Guerrero state, the feminist movement demanded the withdrawal of the Morena candidate for governor, Félix Salgado Macedonio (aka Toro), following accusations of rape and sexual harassment. The body that organises the elections ultimately excluded him, albeit officially for funding irregularities. Local government is often a family affair, however, so the candidate who went on to win the election was his daughter Evelyn, even though she had no political experience. Mexico also had its own #MeToo – with many sectors affected (in the media, for example, three women out of every four said they had been harassed) – and its own Weinstein, who goes by the name of Andrés Roemer. This extremely powerful intellectual and former diplomat was accused by no fewer than sixty-one women, and he fled to Israel to avoid the court cases.

ripping up paving stones, throwing bottles and rocks at the police who were trying to block their path. Many thousands more joined them, understanding the violent nature of the protest, because they were well aware that any one of those smashed windows was considered to be worth more than their lives. Because for the feminist movement in Mexico there is nothing more fundamental or urgent (not employ-ment rights or equal pay or abortion) than their demand: 'Stop killing us.'

Debanhi's father left the press confer-ence and requested an independent autopsy. He could not find the answers he was looking for in the public prosecutor's explanation, let alone in the report stating how his daughter had died. His daughter had not fallen into the water tank by herself. His daughter had been murdered.

Part two of the show started that very day. Debanhi's father had kept back a dark and painful secret. The second autopsy he had requested would unleash all the fears of thousands of women in Mexico.

'If Debanhi Escobar's death was never solved, if there was no justice for such a high-profile case that the whole country had been following, if in this particular case there was at least a body, what could the others hope for?'

They would all be proved right, both the living and the dead. An end had to be put to saying that they all died on their own, that they fell, that they made a mistake. The young girl was buried surrounded by flowers and grief. It looked as if her story would be buried alongside her.

A few days later the Public Prosecutor's Office showed some CCTV videotapes they'd previously said they did not have. These images were recorded inside the motel, very close to the water tank. 'Her final moments of life,' said Guerrero at another sweaty and stuttering press conference. Debanhi running towards the entrance to the motel. Debanhi poking her head into the closed restaurant that was right next to the swimming pool where the water tank was located. They said Debanhi looked upset. Why was she running? Was someone following her? Was she running away from something or someone? The Public Prosecutor's Office could not give any answers to these questions. In the short clips, each of which lasted only a few seconds, no one could be seen other than Debanhi. At this point in the case there was not one single suspect. It was 4.54 in the morning on 9 April. They let everyone imagine the worst. It had to be an accident.

Gustavo Adolfo Guerrero, the public prosecutor, resigned seven months later at the beginning of October. He said he had decided to retire after forty years' service, but no one believed him. The Debanhi case could have been just one more of the dozens of missing women later found dead that he had seen in his career, but the chain of errors, beginning with the search and continuing with an investigation so disastrous that the federal government had to take over to avoid any more embarrassment, was the final blow.

By mid-May doubts were hovering over the case. If Debanhi Escobar's death was never solved, if there was no justice for such a high-profile case that the whole country had been following, if in this particular case there was at least a body (unlike in the cases of thousands of other missing women), what could the others hope for?

The answer lay in Debanhi's body.

'IT IS A VIOLENT DEATH – MURDER'

Very few people had had access to Debanhi's small body. Swollen by the water, it weighed 84.8 kilos. Debanhi was buried one day after the autopsy. This report made no mention of how she had died, simply the cause of death: a blow to her head. There were no details in the first autopsy report explaining whether there had been other blows; whether she may have caused these herself by falling; whether these had happened some time earlier; whether there was evidence of sexual abuse; whether someone else had been involved in her death. The autopsy report raised more doubts than certainties in the case.

The second independent autopsy report raked over everything again. It was a secret report that no one wanted to reveal – until the newspaper *El País* did so. Not even her father, who had meetings with the governor and the public prosecutor and acted as the spokesman in the case. No one mentioned that this document turned everything that had been said about Debanhi to date on its head and that it was included in the files relating to the investigation. She hadn't fallen, it wasn't an accident. She had been murdered.

The second report, to which I had access after covering gender-based violence for eight years in a country that gives no respite to half its population, concluded: 'It is a violent death – murder.' And then everything started all over again, despite efforts made to shelve one of the cases of femicide that had shaken the country most violently.

The coroner who drew up the new autopsy report had no access to Debanhi's body and came to his conclusions simply by examining photographs of different parts of the body and the medical evidence. He also included some significant facts about the mechanics of her death that the first report omitted. In the report he observed that Debanhi Escobar's body 'shows evidence of violent and recent vaginal sexual relations'.

The coroner concluded that the young girl died before her body entered or was thrown into the water tank. He agreed with the first autopsy report on the cause of death being sharp blows to the head, that is 'intracranial haemorrhage resulting in neurogenic shock [damage to the nervous system] leading to respiratory arrest'. The most serious injury, which caused her death, was a sharp blow to the right frontal region of the cranium.

Debanhi's body showed evidence of several injuries to her head, not just one, as the first report seemed to suggest.

'Violet ecchymosis on both sides of the frontal region of the cranium, right and left eyelids, left side of nose, on both lips, above right ear and right retroauricular region,' the document stated. The doctor described the manner of death in the following way: 'The craniofacial contusions are the result of something outside the body and, as they are intense, repeated and with different angles of impact, I conclude that they were caused by another person and that this is a violent death – murder.' The coroner then specified that it must have been with a 'heavy blunt instrument'.

The young girl had not drowned. The water in the tank was ninety centimetres deep, as the authorities had mentioned at the press conference. The coroner remarked that she must have been floating face down as the back of the body was 'dark and dehydrated' compared with the front, which had been 'softened' by the water. However, there was 'no liquid present inside the trachea or the bronchial tubes', so the coroner ruled out death by drowning. 'She was already dead when she entered the water where her body was found.'

Neither did the coroner observe any injuries to her neck, carotid artery or hyoid bone, so he also ruled out death by asphyxiation or strangulation. There was no obstruction to the respiratory orifices or airways resulting from 'thoracoabdominal pressure, interment or confinement', so he also ruled out asphyxiation by suffocation.

Apart from the cause of death mentioned above, another piece of forensic evidence proving that she did not fall is the absence of any fracture or other injuries (apart from those to her head), according to the X-rays that were taken of her corpse. There was, however,

Top to bottom: Three images from Ciudad Juárez: a woman observes the scene of a crime, taking cover behind the door to her house; family members and friends at the funeral of Rosa Isela Escajeda, a young woman who was the victim of a senseless killing; grandmother and granddaughter embrace during the wake for the girl's mother.

> 'It took the Mexican institutions four months to declare a case of a woman's violent death as femicide – 120 days during which any murderer or murderers could flee, hide, destroy evidence, get away with it.'

a fracture present on one nail (an orange acrylic nail): 'a transversal fracture in the middle'.

Debanhi was wearing socks but no shoes, and her torso was partially naked. 'She is wearing a sleeveless white blouse, riding up towards her neck outside the upper-right extremity [right arm] and on the left-hand side, riding up to the left armpit inside the upper-left extremity [left arm],' the report stated.

The second report concluded that she had been murdered and abused. A few months later another autopsy was conducted that ruled out sexual abuse and included another cause of death that the second doctor had excluded: asphyxiation by suffocation.

ONE BODY, TWO AUTOPSIES, NO ARRESTS
The conclusions of the second autopsy report revealed much more than the possible cause of death: the inability of the institutions to conduct a serious investigation at the most basic of levels; furthermore, the attempt to deliberately hide from the public important facts relating to the investigation that contradicted the official theory of an accident. The state Public Prosecutor's Office was going downhill fast.

Given the number of inconsistencies between the first two autopsy reports, the federal government, headed by López Obrador, took over Debanhi's case and promised to exhume her body to conduct a third autopsy. She had spent sixty-eight days in her grave, and all the government had at this point (mid-July) was her body. The result was the same: she had been murdered.

It took the Mexican institutions four months to declare a case of a woman's violent death as femicide – 120 days during which any murderer or murderers could flee, hide, destroy evidence, get away with it. Swell the ranks of the damnable figure of 90 per cent of cases being unsolved.

As I am writing these lines still no one has been arrested or detained for Debanhi's murder, and her case – which focused attention on the horrifying numbers of missing women in the state, which outraged a country that tolerates eleven women being murdered every day – seems doomed never to be afforded justice and the truth. The hopes of thousands of other women who, voiceless and unseen, are murdered with impunity in Mexico are being buried alongside Debanhi.

THE GIRLS' REVOLUTION
They are all Debanhi, her hair wafting in the dark night, these girls who have gathered on the Paseo de la Reforma in Mexico City today. They have not come alone, they are not alone tonight. Their friends are with them, they are looking

At the time the hashtag #MiPrimerAcoso, 'my first attack', was launched on Twitter in 2016, stories about femicides, which are extremely common in Mexico, were still relegated to the crime reports in the media, effectively dismissing the phenomenon as sensationalism. Not that this was the first time that the brutality and frequency of cases of femicide in Mexico had been highlighted. The subject had been covered in Roberto Bolaño's novel *2666*. Compared with the 1990s, however, the part of the country worst afflicted had shifted; it was no longer the northern border with the USA but the heart of the country, Mexico state and above all the city of Ecatepec, which recorded 1,258 women killed between 2015 and 2019. One of the principal causes of this violence is misogyny, rooted in the culture and within all ranks of the local police, in combination with the general corruption in the forces of law and order, which receive federal funding for specific training that too often ends up lining the pockets of local officials. When the AMLO government was publicly asked to act, however, the call was labelled 'opposition propaganda', and the journalist who had put her head above the parapet in the process, Frida Guerrera, was discredited. Yet Guerrera is one of the few who take the trouble to highlight the victims' names and stories and, in some cases, investigate the guilty. The journalist – herself from Ecatepec, a city she left to escape from domestic violence – has assisted in the capture of a number of murderers, some of whom had already been known to the police.

at each other defiantly from behind their balaclavas. Tomorrow they will all be back at school, like any other girl their age, but today they are sharing out cans of petrol and hammers.

Just five years ago the demonstrators only took up a single lane on the Paseo de la Reforma. Now there are tens of thousands of women and girls. The feminist movement in Mexico has become the only opposition to the government of Andrés Manuel López Obrador on the street. López Obrador is one of the most popular presidents in the world and can count on a 60 per cent approval rating. But the feminists (who even the president views as the opposition) are showing their strength at each demonstration, because gender-based violence is still something hanging over this government as it has over all previous governments.

Eleven women are murdered every day in Mexico. The levels of general violence have gone through peaks and troughs, depending on whether a war on drugs (2006–18) has been declared or not, but women and girls are still being murdered without respite. There is a new record every year. That is why there is nothing more pressing as far as Mexican women are concerned. What is more, these crimes are committed with impunity, with the result that there are no consequences whatsoever for those who murder women and girls.

That's why they go out on to the street every International Women's Day on 8 March but also every 25 November, the International Day for the Elimination of Violence Against Women, to protest against gender-based violence, to daub slogans and images on buildings and to put pressure on public opinion, whether in person or online, so that thanks to them every violent death impacts society. Their

A reproduction of a drawing that represents the protest against femicide (*Ni una más*) and about women who have disappeared (*Dónde están*), which is displayed on many walls in central Oaxaca.

'The women are prepared to smash everything to pieces. "Let it ring out loud, we want to live!"'

aim is that no violent death of any woman should be silent, as happened in most cases even five years ago.

The first tipping point occurred with the murders of hundreds of women in Ciudad Juárez in the 1990s. The mothers of the victims managed to get international attention focused on blood-stained Mexico and on this region bordering the United States. Some time later the women murdered in the state of Mexico (the area around the capital city) reminded the country of how little had changed. The rise of the feminist movement worldwide, but particularly since abortion was legalised in Argentina, had an effect in Mexico, and since 2018 each protest march has been immense.

The murdered women are not even counted properly. Not every Mexican state even has the crime of femicide in its criminal code, and, as a result, in many cases, the murders are not even investigated as gender-based violence. The numbers of unreported disappearances may be huge. As at the end of December 2022 the number of reports of missing women since the 1960s – a fraction of the number who have actually disappeared – amounted to more than 28,000, the vast majority of whom have been registered as missing since 2007. No body, no crime. It is one more symptom of a legal system that hasn't even bothered to conduct a clear analysis of the situation and thus enable it to tackle one of the country's greatest tragedies.

They're prepared to smash everything to pieces. 'Let it ring out loud, we want to live!' For Debanhi, Claudia, Esther, Teresa, Ingrid, Fabiola, Valeria. 'I am the girl you grabbed. I am the mother who is mourning her dead girls.' They are gathered around a fire, singing and crying, with what's left of the Paseo and themselves, to see if anyone will listen to them.

Let the state, the skies, the streets tremble
Let the judges and the lawyers tremble
We women are no longer calm today
Fear has been sown, our wings have grown

Every minute of every week
Our friends are stolen, our sisters murdered
They destroy our bodies and make them disappear
Please do not forget their names, Mr President

They refuse to accept that a paving stone is worth more than their lives. That the graffiti painted on the Angel of Independence is investigated more rigorously than their bodies abandoned in gutters. Very few people understand their outrage and their fear.

Fear of going out and not returning home. Clenching your teeth as you turn a corner, clutching your phone, fully aware that it won't be of any use. The primal fear, like that of a hare but without the hare's ability to run at lightning speed in the heat of the chase. How exhausting it is to feel that however fast you run you will always be caught – and that your mother might never find you.

But not tonight. Today, at least, they feel free. 🗡

Tracing Mexico's Complicated Relationship with Rice

Having arrived in Mexico via the Spanish conquest, the presence of rice poses questions as to what's native and what isn't when it comes to a nation's culinary history.

AATISH TASEER

Tourists and locals crowd the restaurants of the famous Mercado 20 de Noviembre in central Oaxaca.

I arrived in Oaxaca on a rainy afternoon in May. We flew over pleated hills that formed a girdle around the Oaxaca valley, one of the most fertile variegated soils in the world. The earth was stamped with cloud shadows that gave an impression both of movement and fixity – a rich, dark earth with an inner seam that showed red and metallic in places. The shadow of the plane, like a fighter escort, followed us as we descended, then was subsumed by the rain-drenched tarmac. The sky was full of light. Leaving the small white airport, we passed a palisade of organ-pipe cactuses. There was blue-leaved agave in the traffic islands and, lining the streets, the trees of my childhood in Delhi – flamboyant laburnum, jacaranda – were in flower. A nondescript modern town of brightly shuttered shops, auto repair and signs that read '*aluminio y vidrio*' gave way to a fully intact Spanish colonial town from the 16th century. 'Downtown: local people,' my driver said, observing the change. '*Centro histórico* for foreign people.'

We came along large-stoned cobbled streets and single-storey buildings painted in warm shades of ochre and that famous Oaxacan colour – a carmine, drawn from the cochineal, a cactus-dwelling insect, which, with the addition of a single drop of lemon juice, turns into one of the most seductive reds known to man. There is no place, not even India, where the use of colour produces as beguiling a mixture of gaiety and melancholy as Mexico. The British writer Rebecca West, who was here in the 1960s, has a description in *Survivors in Mexico* (2003) that cannot be bettered: 'Here these walls are painted colours that are special to Mexico, touching variants of periwinkle blue, a faded acid pink, the terracotta one has seen on Greek vases, a tear-stained elegiac green.'

Speaking of green, there is a green stone of otherworldly beauty known simply as *cantera* that is everywhere in Oaxaca. It appears as exposed quoins on the corners of painted façades. It forms the border of giant grille windows, which, Spanish-style, run the full length of the building. It is there as rustication and entablature – there, too, on one of the city's main churches, Santo Domingo de Guzmán. On that first evening I thought my eyes were deceiving me. The sky had turned half a dozen shades of pink and

AATISH TASEER is the author of several works of fiction and non-fiction. He is a contributing editor at *T* magazine and *Travel and Leisure*. He lives in New York and was most recently the author of *The Twice-Born: Life and Death on the Ganges* (Farrar, Straus and Giroux, USA / Hurst, UK, 2019).

'These were pre-Hispanic ingredients – old Aztec flavours, one imagined – many new to me in texture and taste, and, as such, they felt like an emanation of the culinary history of the land.'

orange before grading into darkness. I walked among captivating scenes of city life – through a first-floor window there were girls out of a Degas painting practising ballet. Opposite was a *mezcalería* with grizzled old men smoking outside. There were baroque theatres and stooped white saints in the tiny alcoves that appeared on high cornerstones. Outside Origen, which belongs to the renowned Oaxacan chef Rodolfo Castellanos – who still works in his restaurant – I pulled out my phone to inspect the exterior. It was not bewitchment or blindness; it was that tender, mournful green.

Inside, in a grand courtyard hung with dried maize whose twirling husks cast starry shadows over the whitewash, itself marked with the Jesuit monogram IHS, symbolising Christ, I ate fried *chapulines* (grasshoppers) as a cocktail snack. A line from Hugh Thomas's *Conquest: Montezuma, Cortés, and the Fall of Old Mexico*, his 1993 history of the subjugation of this land by the Spanish five centuries ago, returned to me. 'Almost everything which moved was eaten,' he wrote of pre-Columbian Mexico. Then, as a tasting menu of several courses unfolded, each bringing with it flavours that were utterly new, I felt intimations of that pre-Columbian past.

We speak so easily of earthiness, of *terroir* and rusticity, but we do not know the meaning of these words until we come to Mexico. In chintextle – a paste made from the pasilla chilli – that had been

smeared on to a tostada of blue corn, I could taste the flavours of the deep earth. It was there again, that volcanic smokiness, in the mole manchamanteles, which, smothering a duck breast, was as red as the soil I had seen from the plane. Death, smoke, desiccation. It was there, too, in the purée of mangrove mussels upon which a piece of striped sea bass appeared. It was as if a portal had been opened to an underworld from which the savour of Mictlán itself (Hades to the Aztecs) flowed out, endowing everything with chthonic force. I half-thought I was losing my mind until a few days later, when Olga Cabrera Oropeza – the chef and founder of Tierra del Sol, a restaurant specialising in moles – confirmed the feeling I had had on that first night in Oaxaca. 'For me,' she said, on a terrace with sweeping views of the emerald city, 'a mole is the presence of dead ingredients that bring a dish to life.' These were pre-Hispanic ingredients – old Aztec flavours, one imagined – many new to me in texture and taste, and, as such, they felt like an emanation of the culinary history of the land.

*

I had come to Mexico in search of what was perhaps the quintessential post-Hispanic ingredient – rice – and, almost immediately, I was confronted by the most reasonable question in the world. '*¿Por qué arroz?*' ('Why rice?'), asked Eduardo 'Lalo' Ángeles, an artisanal mezcal maker with rugged features and sun-scorched skin. Why, in this birthplace of corn, Lalo wanted to know, was I bothering myself about rice? Speaking to me through my guide – Omar Alonso, who sat next to Lalo in a cap for Guerreros de Oaxaca, the local baseball team, under a mural of Mayahuel, the Aztec goddess of maguey (agave) – I heard, in the easy torrent of his Spanish, the word 'Chino'. Omar looked slightly embarrassed, then translated, 'We're not Asian.'

Lalo's surprise piqued my interest. Rice had come to Mexico shortly after the Spanish conquest of the 1520s. It was a time when Spain and Portugal were spreading their tentacles across the globe: the Portuguese viceroy Alfonso de Albuquerque's conquest of Goa, on the west coast of India, occurred nine years before the conquistador Hernán Cortés's 1519 march on Mexico. Some four decades later Spanish vessels known as the Manila Galleons first brought rice to Mexico from the Philippines. What interested me was what place this Old World staple, come via Asia through Europe to the New World, held in the lives of these people who had a mythical attachment to corn. Was it an assimilated part of Mexican food, all memory of its origins forgotten, or was it in some ways still a symbol of the conquest? We assume from a certain kind of Mexican food – the rice-filled tummy of a burrito or the red rice that comes with almost every takeout order – that rice is integral to the cuisine of this country. But the numbers tell a different story: per capita consumption may have increased in recent years – from six kilos in 2011 to almost nine in 2017 – but the average Mexican still only consumes one-fifth as much rice as his coeval in next-door Belize. Mexico does grow some of its own rice for domestic consumption, but the majority

NEW MEXICAN CUISINE

When Cortés arrived in Mexico he found the Aztec Empire at the height of its power after successive conquests had brought a vast territory, stretching as far as Oaxaca in the south, under its control. But Aztec domination of the region lasted only thirty or so years before the arrival of the Spanish, and thus its influence on local populations remained limited. The Central Valleys of Oaxaca were, and are, home to various ethnicities, the most numerous being the Zapotec – who built the famous ruins of Monte Albán – and the Mixtec. The Zapotec population is estimated at being between 400,000 and 650,000 and the Mixtec number some 800,000 (with large communities also present in the USA). While there are restaurants dedicated to regional traditions, 'the new Mexican cuisine' (which is also the title of the 2008 book by the chef Enrique Olvera) takes inspiration from the ingredients, utensils and cooking methods of the whole of pre-Columbian Mexico, without differentiating between regions. For this reason – more than the brief interlude of Aztec control – you will find a mural of Mayahuel, an Aztec (rather than Zapotec or Mixtec) deity in Oaxaca. UNESCO used similar reasoning when it declared the 'traditional' cuisine of the whole of Mexico part of the intangible heritage of humanity (the only national cuisine besides French to make it on to the list), placing the accent on the communal nature of the country's food culture, which emphasises collective participation in the entire chain, from sowing and harvesting the ingredients to the preparation and consumption of the food.

> 'Catholicism – like rice and the knowledge of distillation, which made mezcal possible – had come with the Spanish conquest.'

of its needs, about 70 per cent, are met by imports, mostly from the United States. My interest in the role of rice in Mexico could not be reduced to anything as vulgar as bushels. What intrigued me was the relationship of this grain to the cuisine of this great culinary nation – and what, in turn, that could tell me about Mexico's relationship with its difficult history.

To get to Lalo, Omar and I had driven an hour south from Oaxaca to the small distillery town of Santa Catarina Minas,

set among serried fields of thorn-edged maguey, a squat, potbellied plant with fleshy leaves of a tantalising aquatic green. Above Omar and Lalo, both in their forties, the goddess Mayahuel appeared bare-chested between two fronds of the maguey, gazing dreamily into the distance. All around me were reddish-black piles of timber and fermenting casks of agave. On their surface, amid clouds of insects attracted to the cloying sweetness of sugar turning to alcohol, Lalo had planted tiny bamboo crosses, a mark of his devout Catholicism. Reflecting further on the question – '*¿Por qué arroz?*' – he said that, from his experience, he found that rice was consumed most in places where the Church's influence was strongest.

Packed streets in the historic centre of Oaxaca during the Guelaguetza festival held in July.

'What's the connection between the Church and rice?' I asked Lalo.

'It's an influence from Europe,' he said easily, reminding me of how exotic rice could still seem in Mexico even five hundred years after the Old World's 'discovery' of the Americas.

Catholicism – like rice and the knowledge of distillation, which made Lalo's mezcal possible – had come with the Spanish conquest. That tale of Cortés, the rogue conquistador, who, having burned his boats, subdued the mighty lake-bound capital of the Aztecs, Tenochtitlan – with its 200,000 inhabitants, bigger than any city in Europe, save perhaps Paris – is among the most painful and pitiable episodes in history. With growing horror, one reads of that terrible sequence of events: the first meeting of Cortés and the Aztec emperor Montezuma, one driven by his greed for gold, the other, it was thought – although more recent scholarship has contested this (for example, 'Burying the White Gods: New Perspectives on the Conquest of Mexico' by Camilla Townsend in *The American Historical Review*, June 2003) – labouring under a prophecy that the conquistador was the god Quetzalcoatl reincarnated; the ninety-three-day siege of the lacustrine city, known as the Venice of the New World, which would leave it a burning ruin; the plague-weakened Aztecs, fatally susceptible to Old World diseases such as smallpox, succumbing to the first use of horse and cannon against them. The Spanish triumph, of course, yet one is left feeling a great sense of unease at their victory. As the British neurologist Oliver Sacks wrote in his *Oaxaca Journal* (2002), when confronted by the sheer rapacity of the Spanish melting down of thousands of pre-Columbian gold artefacts at the ruin of Monte Albán in the hills above Oaxaca: 'the conquistadors had showed themselves to be far baser, far less civilised, than the culture they overthrew'. Within half a century of the conquest, Sacks writes, the Aztec population of fifteen million had been reduced to a subjugated three million.

It was during this same period that the Spanish brought rice from Asia, via the port of Acapulco, one of the oldest in Mexico, to their new colony, where the soil and climate were suitable for its cultivation. This movement of goods and technology, by which the Old and New Worlds literally seeded one another, is known as the Columbian Exchange, which had started decades before in Spanish colonies in the Caribbean – including Cuba, Hispaniola and Puerto Rico – but which had been taken to new heights after the conquest of Mexico. To the Old World there flowed such indispensable things as maize, chocolate, chillies, tomatoes, avocados, potatoes and rubber. The Americas, in turn, received the wheel, the horse, sugar, wheat, livestock, a syllabic script and, of course, rice. The changes the Columbian Exchange wrought are so profound, so embedded now in our way of life, that it is hard to imagine the world before them. It boggles the mind to think of India, where I grew up, as not having chillies until only five centuries ago. Or Italy and Greece doing without tomatoes. As the Mexican writer Octavio Paz, who had served as ambassador to India, puts it in *Itinerary: An Intellectual Journey* (1980): 'The discovery of America initiated the planet's unification.'

But, as we already know, the conquest of Mexico was not a benign affair. Here there was no mere happy exchange of exotic fruit. It left a layered society, full of unresolved historical pain. 'The nations of ancient Mexico,' Paz writes, 'lived in constant war, one against the other, but it

While rice in Mexico is still an interloper, the same cannot be said of the many foods from the Americas that arrived in the Old World following the Columbian Exchange. Of all these, the least conspicuous, but by far the most important, is maize, also known as corn, which originated in central Mexico. It is more widespread in Asia than you might imagine, and it continues to spread. More maize is produced in China – the world's second largest producer after the USA – than rice or any other cereal, and Indonesia and India are in the top ten ahead of Mexico itself. Maize is the world's second most widely cultivated crop after sugarcane, and its production has tripled in the space of forty years. The reason for this breathtaking growth is not that the whole world has started eating tacos, it is because maize is perhaps the best example of what are known as flex crops – as with soya and palm oil, it's not just about food. When made into bioethanol it fuels vehicles and machines. The starch and sugar it produces are found in processed foods and myriad everyday products – paints, textiles, wallpaper, soap, candles, newspapers, cigarettes, insecticides, dry-cell batteries, cosmetics, plastic, nitroglycerine, fireworks, shoe polish – but, above all, it is used in industrial quantities as animal feed, and, given the trends in meat and fish consumption in Asia, it can only become more vital in the near future. While it is difficult to imagine pizzas without tomato or curries without chilli, the contemporary world without maize really is inconceivable.

was only with the arrival of the Spaniards that they really faced the other, that is, a civilisation different from their own.' That sentence, *mutatis mutandis*, could have been written about India, where Islamic invasions and British rule still produced an anxiety about authenticity – what was one's own, what had come from outside. I was interested in that anxiety, which could manifest itself both in tangible and intangible ways.

'*¿Por qué arroz?*' indeed. I guess I hoped rice, like dye in a chemistry experiment, would serve me as a flow tracer of sorts – a way to enter the complexities of Mexico's past through something as concrete as food.

*

'Rice is not filling,' Lalo said. 'If you eat it, then after two or three hours in the fields you're hungry again. If you have beans, you can hang on longer.'

Omar laughed, in part, I thought, because Lalo seemed to take the intrusion of the crop in his birthplace so personally.

'Think about it,' Lalo said. 'When was the last time you cooked rice in your house?'

Omar nodded. 'It's a restaurant thing.'

'But horchata? All the time.'

Lalo and Omar spoke to an element of novelty that rice still possesses in this part of Mexico, its tapered southern end surrounded by rice-producing states such as Tabasco, Campeche and Veracruz. The presence of the crop was remarkable enough for Lalo to associate it with the Church, which was inseparable from the conquest. Omar linked it to the more artificial setting of a restaurant, as opposed to what one made at home, reminding me that this was one of those countries, like India and China, where restaurant food was a cuisine apart from what one ate in

Above: The up-and-coming Oaxaca chef Thalía Barrios García in the garden of La Cocina de Humo, one of her two restaurants, both of which specialise in using local ingredients in traditional Oaxaqueña cuisine.
Right: Inside La Cocina de Humo.

'But if there is one point of contact, one aperture through which the Mexico of today can reach out its fingers and touch the Aztec past, it is food.'

people's houses. And later I would meet another chef who would trace its origins in her life to a government food-security scheme. All of which is to say that rice, although partially assimilated, still felt somehow alien. (To give you a sense of the disparity, in 2018 Mexico consumed a paltry 1.2 million tonnes of rice, whereas a rice-eating nation of roughly equal size, like Japan, say, consumed over seven million.) But, as the basis for horchata, it was perfectly natural. The drink – a cold, cloudy, sweet liquid exalted by the presence of fruits and nuts – has an ancient origin in North Africa. It came to the Iberian Peninsula via the Moorish conquest of Spain in the 8th century. Known then, too, for its cooling quality, it was made with tiger nuts, but when these failed to make it aboard the ships of

conquistadors, horchata was reborn in the New World with a new basis in rice, still carrying on the fight against the stultifying heat of a day like today.

Before our trip to the distillery, Omar and I had been in the tiny Oaxacan village of Santo Tomás Jalieza, a place of large-leaved verdure, corrugated-steel fencing and tropical lanes of red earth with puddles that reflected the vacant intensity of the Mexican sky. There, at the house of the Navarro sisters, three unmarried weavers in their fifties, Omar and I had witnessed a rarity even in Mexico: horchata made from scratch. In a shaded courtyard overgrown with succulents, Margarita, with her greying pigtails and brightly embroidered apron, had crushed rice, which had been soaking for an hour or so, on a *metate*, a hollowed, mortar-like stone. Nearby, Inés, stouter but dressed similarly – in a brown dress and apron, on which there sprawled bright blue and red flowers – prepared all that would go into the horchata: melon, walnut, red-fleshed prickly pear. Back and forth Margarita went, mashing the rice to gruel. Now and then she flicked bits of cinnamon on to the pocked ashen surface of the *metate*. The mashed rice turned a pale brown. When enough had collected in the clay pot at the edge of the quern, the two sisters – the third Navarro sister, Crispina, was an amused bystander – squeezed out its impurities using a wet cloth. Margarita added sugar, ice and all the condiments. In a round-bottomed gourd, beautifully painted with a bright-red ground covered in leaves and flowers, the hemisphere bifurcated by a white-flecked band of superb Mexican blue, which, in turn, sat on a glazed clay cup, I was presented with my first horchata.

On that hot afternoon, the throbbing blue tent of sky above me, it was magically refreshing, full of surprise and fragrance, the drab, ice-cold graininess of its texture transformed by the inclusion of bright fruits and the gritty richness of nuts. It was also a million miles away from any previous notion I'd had of rice. It felt like what in artistic circles is described as a response – as if the New World, desperately bored by the prospect of rice, had souped it up with every possible bell and whistle, so that almost nothing remained of the interloping grain that had tried to muscle its way over to the Americas on the boats of the conquistadors. I drank it down, then drank another.

Swimming back into myself, I saw Omar and Lalo sitting against the turmeric-coloured wall where Mayahuel held sway. Thinking of India, where the old gods, despite centuries of conquest, had not been overthrown, I wondered if it was easy for Lalo to balance his regard for the Aztec pantheon with his allegiance to the Church.

'For us, no,' he said, without so much as a glance back at Mayahuel, whose smoky nectar we had been consuming in voluminous quantities, 'because we are the product of the conquest.'

*

The next day, under the 'blue uneasy alkaline sky' of D.H. Lawrence's 'Mornings in Mexico' (1927), Omar and I, at the Mercado de Abastos – a warren of shaded lanes, no wider than corridors, with sleek, undulating walls of corrugated steel and work tables dressed brightly in their oilcloths – walked among the ingredients I had tasted

that first night in Oaxaca at Origen. As I'd learned the day before, the pre-conquest past, in areas such as language (Náhuatl), religion (an earth religion where the obsidian knife was routinely used in human sacrifice), dress ('the upper class', writes Thomas in *Conquest*, wore robes of long quetzal feathers, and very elaborate cloaks of white duck feathers, embroidered skirts and necklaces with radiating pendants) and architecture (great stepped pyramids rising out of a lake encircled by volcanoes), has all but gone under in Mexico. But if there is one point of contact, one aperture through which the Mexico of today can reach out its fingers and touch the Aztec past, it is food. And that past, here at the Mercado de Abastos, through the prevalence of corn, cacao and chillies – and the absence of rice – could still feel very present.

'I don't like to plan,' Omar said waspishly that morning over a café con piquete – a coffee with a stinging shot of mezcal – in Enrique Olvera's restaurant Criollo. (Olvera is Mexico's original rock-star chef, with such establishments as Pujol in Mexico City and Cosme in New York to his name.) Thanks to Omar, we were served up an impromptu feast. Conchas, a sweet Mexican corn bread with an even layer of charred husk, which I was meant to dunk in my coffee. Rib-eye soup. A taco of beef, chorizo and quesillo (string cheese). Another with berros (fragrant greens) and a salsa of chicharrones (fried pork skin). All this, I should add, was merely a prelude to the morning of street food Omar had arranged. Observing me quail at the prospect of more, he plied me sadistically with an enmolada whose red mole contained the rarest, most expensive of all chillies: chilhuacle – stout, triangular and of impossible smokiness.

'Oaxappiness!' Omar proclaimed.

And then we were off – Omar playing Ariadne to my Theseus – through a street of prostitutes, preening in the clear morning air, deep into the cool labyrinth of the market. I had been in markets all my life, in places as far apart as Ouarzazate and Luang Prabang, Samarkand and Kigali, but that was the Old World. Here, in this New World market, one felt the ubiquity of the absence of Old World produce like rice, and my reaction was not unlike that of Columbus himself first setting eyes on the newness of the New World: 'I saw neither sheep nor goats nor any other beast' – he writes in his journals – 'but I have been here a short time, half a day; yet if there were any I couldn't have failed to see them … There were dogs that never barked … All the trees were as different from ours as day from night, and so the fruits, the herbage, the rocks and all things.' It was amazing how, on that morning, a sense of New World wonder still prevailed after the passage of five centuries. Dizzying varieties of chilli rose around me in steep escarpments of roach-like red verging on black. I now knew pasilla and chilhuacle, but did I know that there were two varieties of the latter? And what of other chilli varieties such as guajillo, cascabel *and* morita? Omar was relentless, pressing on through the tented streets scalloped with pools of sunlight. Sometimes he would stop to buy a delicacy, like huitlacoche – corn that had sprouted an efflorescence of rich blue fungus. We took the corn smut to Doña Vale, an elderly lady whose memelas – a thick pre-Hispanic tortilla – and salsa of tomatillos (a green fruit also known as the Mexican husk tomato) had made her a TV star when she was featured on the Netflix series *Street Food*. When we found her, she was in a cerise dress ornamented with black lace, two carmine stones in her ears, flanked by a couple of loutish youths in masks and hoodies taking selfies. In a gesture of friendship, Omar gave her the smut, and we plunged deeper into the market, where a 36-year-old woman named Mago, also famous for her memelas, stood ready to make us our umpteenth breakfast. Young and vivacious, in a green-camouflage T-shirt, she threw a couple of hierba santa leaves on a hot *comal* (a flat griddle), where they wilted instantly, and began to cook eggs over them. In between cooking for us, Mago pressed tortillas between two sheets of orange plastic on a blue metal press from which the paint flaked. The band Grupo Soñador, known for its Mexican take on the Latin American folk music cumbia, played a brassy, jaunty number in the background from a speaker. Omar crushed an avocado on to the wilted leaves, scattering guaje seeds on it – a vine grass that grows in the surrounding hills, and from which the word 'Oaxaca' itself is derived. All around me, from the sight of a woman standing in the distance, with strong Indian features and pigtails, a basket of nopales (cactuses) on her head, to men offering me pulque, a pre-Hispanic drink made from the fermented sap of the

'Dizzying varieties of chilli rose around me in steep escarpments of roach-like red verging on black. I now knew pasilla and chilhuacle … And what of other chilli varieties?'

maguey, I saw the vestiges of a past that, although worn thin in places, was full of novelty. It was against this newness that rice felt almost like a memory of the Old World – a world elsewhere.

*

On my last day in Oaxaca, Omar took me to Levadura de Olla, a restaurant whose name means 'the yeast of the cooking pot'. It had been started by a 26-year-old chef named Thalia Barrios García, who came from San Mateo Yucutindoo, a village in the Sierra Sur, the hills surrounding Oaxaca. She was kneading three kinds of maize when we came in. One of the joys of being in Oaxaca, unlike other food capitals, was how close the connection still was between fine cuisine and the traditions people had grown up with. Thalia's aunts and grandmother had all been cooks. She had learned from them.

A government agency with the acronym CONASUPO – which provided food security to economically disadvantaged areas – had introduced *arroz* to Thalia's village in the mid-1980s. 'Rice is something you eat with tortillas before you go to work in the fields,' she said, taking us back to the idea of the staple as a raw source of energy and sustenance in agrarian communities. Lalo had said something similar but with the opposite meaning: rice, he felt, was poor sustenance; beans were better. But what surprised me, watching her make *arroz rojo* (red rice) and *arroz con frijoles* (rice and beans), was how recent that introduction had been. Lalo had traced a line to the Church; Thalia now traced one to a government agency. It made rice seem so foreign, so new, in a way that I could never imagine a Punjabi farmer in north India, consuming a corn roti and spinach on a cold winter's morning, ever feeling. Obviously, we in the Old World had assimilated the New World far more unthinkingly than was true in reverse. In a beautiful green glazed pot, which sat on a wood-fired *comal*, Thalia was blackening a few costeño chillis. To these, from a clay *sartén*, or pan, she added the softest, mashiest frijoles I had ever seen, then diluted the mixture with water. It was now a soup of sorts, into which Thalia sprinkled salt, avocado leaves and, of course, *arroz*.

It was the best thing I ate in Oaxaca. In its raw, terrestrial graininess, it reminded me of dishes, like dal (lentils) and rice in India, that are pared down to a simplicity so perfect that even the addition of salt can feel like a flourish. Soon other things arrived: five kinds of tomatoes overlaying a beetroot purée. Mezcal. Then an offspring of the rain, which now came every afternoon like clockwork – a mole of chicatanas.

'Chicatanas?' I asked Omar.

'Flying ants,' he replied dryly.

*

'In exile, food becomes important,' the ex-*shahbanu* of Iran had once told me in Morocco, where I was on an assignment for *The New York Times*. Mexico, in many ways, is a country exiled from its pre-Hispanic past. As with Iran and the Arab conquest of the seventh century, the pain of what had been lost was still fresh centuries after. Considering the nature of Mexico's 'inner conflict', Paz wrote, 'I found that it was the result of a historical wound buried in the depths of the past'.

On that last night in Oaxaca, the reverberations of that wound came to the surface. I sat on a terrace, overlooking dark cobblestones bathed in yellow streetlight, with a young dancer by the name of Enrique. He had a light beard, fine features, and his slight, slim body vibrated with the historical anger that the conquest

A fruit-and-vegetable stall outside the Mercado 20 de Noviembre in the historic centre of Oaxaca.

could still produce in Mexico. 'By the end of the conquest,' Enrique said, 'the people who had the power were the white people. Even the revolutions were led by white people.'

The legacy of that conquest, as Matthew Restall argues in *When Montezuma Met Cortés: The True Story of the Meeting that Changed History* (2018), was taken up by the United States once Spanish power had failed on the American mainland. In two friezes on the rotunda of the US Capitol building in Washington, DC, a clear parallel is drawn between Montezuma's surrender to Cortés and the Mexican general Santa Anna's surrender to the United States after the Mexican–American War of 1846–8.

'Every country has its phantoms,' writes Paz, no doubt thinking of the war that cost Mexico half its territory. 'France for the Spaniards, Germany for the French, ours have been Spain and the United States.' Paz goes on to describe Mexico's neighbour to the north as a reality 'so vast and powerful that it borders on myth', producing a relationship on Mexico's end that is 'polemical and obsessive'. How could it not be? The United States' gaze, even before Trump's talk of Mexicans as rapists and criminals, was corrosive, turning this country with its rich, layered history, into little more than a brutish source of labour. Enrique himself worked part-time as farm labourer on a plantation in California that grew not rice but marijuana. And that relationship felt exploitative – as it had been for Omar, who crossed the US border illegally when he was eighteen and lived and worked in Los Angeles restaurants for the next decade.

Enrique, in turn, lived with his own sense of historical unease. He was neither white nor Indigenous. Like over half of Mexico, he was mestizo, of mixed blood, a child of the conquest. He privileged the authenticity of a pure Indigenous Mexico over the mestizo country in which he lived, relaying the crimes of the colonisers. As he spoke, I was reminded of a moment in *Survivors in Mexico* when West is confronted with a similar situation with a taxi driver in Mexico City. 'The man,' she writes, 'is not identifying some monstrous invader of his people's lands, as Poles might denounce the Nazi Germans; he is denouncing some of his ancestors for maltreating other of his ancestors, which, as he is both, must lead to schizophrenia.'

The emanations of that schizophrenia had been with me throughout my time

Taking a nap in front of a restaurant counter inside Oaxaca's Mercado de la Merced.

in Mexico. I had come among people who had been remade by the Spanish conquest but who had battled within themselves on behalf of a truer, Indigenous Mexico. When I asked Enrique to pick out the people who were Indigenous, he said, 'They're not here. They're on the street, begging for money or selling candy, but they're not here. They're somewhere else.'

Their absence, symbolising the loss of old Mexico, was pain. On this epicurean journey in Oaxaca, I had seen food serve as a way for people to commune with that vanquished past. It was a rare line of continuity that ran from the pre-Columbian era into the Mexican present, allowing the society to glimpse a shattered wholeness.

But, as much as people suffered on account of their histories, their relationship to food tells a different story, speaking always of our talent for assimilation and absorption. '*¿Por qué arroz?*' Lalo had asked. The answer was plain: the Columbian Exchange was proof like no

From cradle to grave, Coca-Cola is a constant companion in Mexico. This is especially true in Chiapas, which has the world's highest per capita consumption; there it makes its first appearance in babies' bottles, is offered to the gods and even serves as an informal currency with which to pay fines or ask for a girl's hand in marriage. There have long been very close ties with the multinational. The first president of the democratic era, Vicente Fox, was previously head of Coca-Cola Mexico, which currently employs 100,000 people, although it is indirectly responsible for more than a million jobs and 1.4 per cent of the country's GDP. Since at least the 2000s, however, there has been a clear understanding of the correlation between heavy consumption of sugary drinks, which many link to Mexico joining NAFTA (see 'The Worst Trade Deal …' on page 86), and the increase in obesity with its severe health implications, which result in an estimated 40,000 Mexican deaths per year. Three-quarters of Mexicans are considered overweight, and the growth in cases of diabetes has been out of control for decades, so politicians have been forced to take action, in spite of conflicts of interest. In 2014 Mexico became one of the first countries in the world to introduce a tax on carbonated drinks, which slightly lowered the consumption curve. In 2020 this was followed by a requirement to add a label to foods with a high sugar content, and the same year the state of Oaxaca made history with its ban on selling junk food to children. For kids in Oaxaca it might well be easier to get their hands on a shot of tequila than a sweet snack!

other of how, when it comes to food, so often the venue of our greatest nativisms, we, as human beings, easily slip the ties of belonging. No man dipping his satay in peanut sauce in Bangkok, or woman eating chicken paprikash in Budapest, or any number of families consuming potatoes across the breadth of Russia, stops for one moment to consider how relatively recently these seminal ingredients have been added to their national cuisines, even if, like Enrique, those same people still bristle from the after-effects of conflicts that are centuries old. We apply the terms 'invasive' and 'native' to the vegetable kingdom. They are full of resonance for us, but every day, at our dining tables, we set aside our obsession with origins – what is ours, what has come from outside – nourishing ourselves on an endlessly fertile encounter with the other. 🐦

Mother, Mole and Pujol:

A Microhistory of Mexican Cuisine

RENATA LIRA

Mexican cuisine is an ephemeral concept. We believe that we understand what it is, but, when we try to describe it, words escape us. We are never entirely convincing, fair or comprehensive – like the self-evolving, unattainable character of human experience that Ralph Waldo Emerson analyses in his 1841 essay 'Circles', describing it as a 'self-evolving circle, which, from a ring imperceptibly small, rushes on all sides outwards to new and larger circles, and that without end'. It is surely no coincidence then that the most iconic dish at Mexico's most famous top-end restaurant has the same circular, evolving form. I am referring to Pujol's *mole madre*, a dish comprised of two different mole sauces plated in concentric circles: a freshly made

red (or *coloradito*) mole in the centre of the plate surrounded by a black Oaxacan mole that has been reheated every day since 2013. The mother and the son. Wisdom and evolution. If the success of Pujol's chef Enrique Olvera could be summed up in one dish, it would be this; if the story of Mexican cuisine could be told with a single dish, it would also be not only *this* mole but *all* moles repeating themselves in a circle ad infinitum.

If we classify the ingredients of every mole, simply through repetition we can decipher their primary components. Also, if we separate each one out and trace its origin we can discern the influences of other cultures on our own. There are dishes that through their origins lay bare the history of the people. Mole exemplifies this well. We do not know when it was first prepared, but we do know that by the time the conquistadors arrived in Mexico it was already a ceremonial dish. In his *Historia*

RENATA LIRA is a Mexican author and cook. She has written for, among others, *Apart*, *Letras libres*, *Hoja santa*, *Frente* and contributed to *Comer relaciona (y confronta) mundos* for the Centro Cultural de España in Mexico. She writes about food in the *Atole Newsletter*.

general de las cosas de la Nueva España (1540–85), Fray Bernardino de Sahagún describes chilli stews, or *chilmollis*, that were prepared with various chillies, tomatoes, pumpkin seeds, masa flour, roast and ground beans, the herbs *hoja santa* and *epazote*, avocado leaf and unripe plums, which were served in casseroles to accompany turkey, frogs, tadpoles, axolotls, fish, lobster, shrimp, winged ants, maguey worms, wild mushrooms and *quelites* (wild greens).

Later, in convents as well as Criollo homes, ingredients from Europe and Asia began to find their way into these dishes. In *The Moles: Pre-Hispanic Contributions*, Cristina Barros discovers fragments of recipe books that show their evolution: that of Dominga Guzmán (1750) with a *pipián* (green mole) with sesame and peanuts; that of Fray Gerónimo de San Pelayo (1780) with a *manchamanteles* (stew) flavoured with cumin; a *clemole* (soup) from the *Recetario novohispano* (1791) with roasted sesame, coriander, cumin, garlic, cloves, pepper, cinnamon and ginger (here we can start to see the relationship with curry that Octavio Paz discussed in *In Light of India*); and another *clemole* in the *Arte novísimo de la cocina* (1872) in which cocoa appears for the first time in a Mexican recipe.

So, how did we move from *ceremonial* moles to *tasting-menu* moles?

A number of historical processes led to the place in which we find ourselves today. The practice of eating out is very old, initially out of necessity and later exalted as a pleasure, and although this shift in mindset is not particular to any time or culture, the French concept of the *restaurant* was the first to institutionalise it. The original restaurants were literally – as discussed by Rebecca L. Spang in her book *The Invention of the Restaurant* – places where one could be 'restored'. Before this concept of wellness and that of the à-la-carte restaurant that the French exported to the world in the 19th century, two important transformations took place: the French Revolution and the period of Napoleonic rule.

The pleasure of good eating ceased to be a privilege reserved for the courtly elites, but the new gastronomic philosophy was not exactly built on the ideals of equality. Eating at a restaurant became such a sophisticated activity that its language became incomprehensible to most people. Two elements then appeared to help interpret this new narrative: menus and food critics. The first facilitated a better dialogue between diners and the kitchen; the latter – ironically – made it more inaccessible and elitist. Figures such as Jean Anthelme Brillat-Savarin and Grimod de la Reynière became popular. In 1803 de la Reynière published the first edition of *L'Almanach des gourmands*, an important work, considering its gastronomic-literary content, but one that is the antecedent of a pernicious virus from which the restaurant industry still suffers today: the guides, the stars, the lists, the 'star' chefs and all those arbitrary and inequality-fostering recognition systems.

The arrival of the French restaurant model in Mexico also took place in the context of two key transformations: the Porfiriato of the late 19th and early 20th centuries and the Mexican Revolution of 1910–20. The ruling elite clearly favoured the *European* over the *Indigenous*, and the restaurants and their language only served to further accentuate these class tensions. Following the Revolution the country remained socially and politically divided, but the opposite was hapenning in the country's kitchens. If we open an older cookbook – *El cocinero mexicano* ('Mexican

Cooking'), for example – we can see that before the French-style restaurant arrived in Mexico there was already a fusion cuisine that found its best expression in the convents. *Chiles en nogada* (stuffed chillies) are an excellent example of this *mestizaje*, or cultural mix.

After the uprising, this parallel culinary revolution continued to develop thanks to the activities of domestic cooks – led in large part by Josefina Velázquez de León and Vicenta Torres Rubio – who got together in groups to produce a series of cookbooks in which, according to Jeffrey M. Pilcher in *Qué Vivan los Tamales! Food and the Making of Mexican Identity* (University of New Mexico Press, 1998), middle-class women 'expressed their personal visions of the nation, while maintaining an air of domestic respectability'. This task of collecting the culinary memory of women from all over the country turned out to be the only truly effective way to incorporate the plurality of Mexico and build a sense of community and identity among the people, something that the actual Revolution had failed to do. This continuity of the role of women in the culinary life of the nation has never been lost, although in the world of chefs and restaurants it remains largely invisible.

In an interview published in 2016 in the Mexican literary magazine *Letras libres*, Enrique Olvera discusses what influenced him creatively in the 1980s and 1990s. 'In Mexico there were no "great chefs", if anything, there were great restaurants … My references were what my mother cooked. My mum's handwritten recipe book,' he says, which seems a little disingenuous given that by then there were already a few well-known figures – cooks, restaurateurs, authors, television hosts, teachers, some of whom were all of these – such as Josefina Velázquez de León,

Patricia Quintana, Mónica Patiño, Alicia Gironella, Carmen Ramírez Degollado and Carmen Ortuño to mention a few. The fact that he highlights his mother's recipe book as his only culinary reference says more than it seems, because, albeit unintentionally, it reveals the lack of recognition that the influence of women's cooking is afforded in the professional arena, when, in truth, this is precisely where it comes from, that it is from there that he himself drew his greatest ideas. That kind of Mexican cuisine – prepared in homes, in the countryside and in the streets – is one that has never stopped evolving. It is old and wise but at the same time modern and inclusive. It is not prejudiced or snobbish. It makes use of what is available and is no stranger to modernity. It incorporates. It adds. It's like a glass of *esquites* (corn kernels) with mayonnaise, lime and chilli powder – another iconic classic that can be found reinterpreted on the menu at Pujol.

In that same interview Olvera identifies three key stages in his cooking journey: first, the influence of Thomas Keller's new Californian cuisine; next, a deconstruction of Mexican cuisine along the lines of the model found at Ferran Adrià's El Bulli in Spain; finally, a simplicity inspired by René Redzepi at Noma in Copenhagen. If we take a look at a recent Pujol menu we will spot several things. The first is that – as noted by Dan Jurafsky in *The Language of Food: A Linguist Reads the Menu* (W.W. Norton, 2014) – it is generally the case these days that the more expensive the restaurant is, the fewer options one has. In that regard, Pujol's menu is somewhere in the middle: six courses offering three options per course, except the first and fifth (the *antojitos* – appetisers – and the mole), which are fixed. It does reflect that cult-like tendency for the figure of the chef/author to make decisions on behalf

of the diner, but it also allows a degree of flexibility. We can also identify a regional approach, not in a strict sense, but one that favours native ingredients: heirloom corn, chayote, runner beans, chillies, greens such as *romeritos* and *quintoniles*, tomatillos, prickly pear, wild mushrooms ... The menu is mostly vegetarian, another aspect taken from pre-Hispanic cuisine. We can also identify a number of more personal elements: a memory of the *calamares en su tinta* (squid in ink) from his mother's recipe book in the 'octopus in habanero ink with runner beans and salsa veracruzana'; or the sauce with chicatana ants ground in a mortar and pestle that he tried in Cuquila, Oaxaca, mixed with Mexico's favourite street snack in the 'tender corn with coffee mayonnaise and chicatana ants'. (The Netflix series *Chef's Table* dedicated an episode to Olvera, in which a number of his dishes feature.)

The French philosopher and author Jean-François Revel said that Mexican cuisine was a product not of art but of ethnography; he also said that international haute cuisine was superior to all others because the chefs who practise it are men. Such ideas, which today sound archaic and rather absurd, have not, in fact, been completely eradicated. Women in restaurant kitchens in Mexico are still found in secondary roles, as spectators, aspirants or sidekicks rather than *true* creators, and yet it is they who keep all the traditional wisdom. On the other hand, superfluous and ambiguous meanings are often given to adjectives such as *authentic* and *sophisticated* when applied to food.

A woman collecting corn in the field, putting it out to dry, shucking it, separating it, boiling it with the exact proportions of water and lime, by smell and touch knowing the cooking and resting times, cleaning and rinsing the corn between her fingers, taking it to the mill or grinding it on a *metate*, kneading it into a soft dough that she flattens with the palms of her hands until it forms a thin and even circle that, in one practised movement, she lays deftly on the *comal*, and which, after being turned a couple of times, puffs up into a perfect sphere: that's art. If we can give Olvera credit for anything, it is for convincing more people – Mexicans included – that it really *is* art. But such a thing would not have happened without his mother's recipe book, without the unconditional support of his wife and without the wisdom of millions of Mexican *cocineras*.

This is not about taking anything away from Olvera. What I want to say is that the reality of the culinary world – like so many others – is that it is still in large part dominated by a patriarchal model, and that it took a man who graduated from an elite US cookery school to drive the world mad for a Mexican dish. Pujol's *mole madre* is nothing if not a reflection of the times in which we live, and if its value lies in anything, it is in that each bite of corn tortilla and *hoja santa* covered in mole – half *old,* half *new* – is, in reality, a tribute to the deep, rustic, Indigenous, conventual, Creole, European, Asian, Middle-Eastern, revolutionary, street, domestic and feminine cuisine: the mother of all moles.

The Pearl of the West

Guadalajara and Jalisco in the words of a writer who fell in love with Mexico in the 1980s – and has never stopped talking about it.

PINO CACUCCI
Translated by Oonagh Stransky

A blossom-filled street with a view of the
parish church of Tequila, the town not
far from Guadalajara that gives its name
to the famous spirit.

All the road trips that I have ever taken in Mexico share one initial challenge: getting out of the capital city. It can take hours to make your way through the heavy traffic that clogs the streets at all times – and it was worse back when we didn't have GPS. By 'back when' I mean the early 1980s, when I travelled to Guadalajara with a group of friends in a beaten-up VW van, which in Mexico they still call Combis. Ours looked like a relic from a long-lost era. Yellow and white, it had had four or five previous owners and even sported California licence plates. When we reached the end of the Carretera, the Federal Highway, after crossing through the state of Hidalgo and into Queretaro, it felt like the hardest part of the trip was over. But we still had four hundred kilometres to travel, down patched-up asphalt roads that – whether they passed through cities, towns, villages or just small clusters of shacks – were punctuated with endless *topes*, those awful speed bumps that will destroy a car's suspension if you don't come to a complete halt.

On those early long journeys, brimming with the enthusiasm of twenty-year-olds, we quickly came to understand why Mexicans choose not to express themselves in kilometres but in time. It doesn't make sense to say that the trip from Mexico City to Guadalajara is 550 kilometres; it all depends on the kind of road you're on, which towns you choose to pass through and so on. In Mexico it's all about how and when you travel. Back then, just like today, people would recommend you didn't travel at night. Putting aside potential hold-ups, in the dark it's hard to avoid wandering cows and horses and even the occasional deer.

Back in the early 1980s motorways were pretty much non-existent and those that had been built fell far short of our concept of 'thoroughfares for fast-moving vehicles'. Mexico is filled with reminders that speed – in all shapes, manners and forms – only serves to get you into the grave faster. It is slowness that's the key to understanding *mexicanidad*, the philosophy of taking life at a more relaxed pace so you can enjoy it more fully and for an extended length of time. Foreigners often struggle to understand and accept this, causing them to spin out with anxiety and do things less well and less efficiently.

After leaving Guanajuato and entering

PINO CACUCCI is an author, screenwriter and translator whose work has traced a path between travel literature, crime fiction, historical novels, theatre, cinema and graphic novels. He has published more than twenty titles, including *Puerto Escondido* (1990), which was adapted into a film by Gabriele Salvatores, *Tina* (1991), *San Isidro Futból* (1991), which was filmed as *Viva San Isidro!*, *La polvere del Messico* (1992), *Viva la vida!* (2010), *Mujeres* (2018) – a graphic novel with Stefano Delli Veneri – and *L'elbano errante* (2022). Works published in English include *Without a Glimmer of Remorse* (2005) and *The Whales Know* (2014).

the state of Jalisco, the horizon before us was suddenly filled with the blue-green colour of the agave plant, which is used to make tequila. The fields stretched as far as the eye could see. The plant, deeply sacred to the Maya and Aztecs, is now the source of precious liquor ... for the entire world. As extensive as the fields are, it's hard to believe that the millions of litres of tequila that make their way around the globe come from Jalisco alone.

Since that first trip to Guadalajara, back when we looked at things with eyes wide open, I have returned on multiple occasions, and the more I learned about contemporary Guadalajara – an elegant and wealthy city in all senses of the word – the more I became fascinated by its history.

*

A worker prepares the *piñas* obtained from the agave plant, which will be used to make tequila.

It was the year of Our Lord 1532. The adventurers who followed in the footsteps of Hernán Cortés were busily scouring the immense territories of Nueva España for riches and wealth that would eventually change, within just a few decades, not only the history of Castilian Spain but that of the whole of Europe. Many conquistadors, who had once been skilled seafarers, became armigers against their will, others had their own particular reasons for steering clear of the law of the Crown, while hidalgos of truly noble lineage were few and far between. One of them was Nuño Beltrán de Guzmán, who was born in the Spanish town of Guadalajara northeast of Madrid; if anyone was living proof that a person's noble lineage could be inversely proportional to nobility of spirit, it was him. The man was stubborn, power-hungry and so cruel that he tortured to death Tangaxoan, the wise monarch of the Purépecha, who had converted to Christianity and had no hidden treasure at

At the eastern end of the historic centre of Guadalajara stands the Hospicio Cabañas, an immense neoclassical building designed to house poor and orphaned children. The chapel in the complex boasts fifty-seven murals by the Jalisco painter José Clemente Orozco. Since 1983 it has been the home of the Instituto Cultural Cabañas, which, in four decades of activity, has established itself as the most important cultural hub in the city of Guadalajara.

'Beltrán de Guzmán harboured a dream. He wanted to found a city and name it Guadalajara after the town of his birth. Perhaps he felt nostalgia for his homeland.'

all. That same year Beltrán de Guzmán's heartless deeds triggered such a violent outcry from the clergy of Pátzcuaro (now in the state of Michoacán) that he was formally dismissed as president of the Primera Audiencia de la Nueva España. This came as a bitter blow to the ambitious 42-year-old conquistador, who was also a bitter rival of Cortés, who had himself been stripped of his own rank of capitán general after a dispute with Beltrán de Guzmán in 1529.

Once Cortés was back in power Beltrán de Guzmán feared retribution, so he decided to *poner tierra por medio* and get as far away as possible to seek out new conquests. With a personal army of three hundred Spaniards and six hundred Indigenous slaves (the Caribbean slave trade was one of his main sources of income), he set his sights on the north-west, unafraid either of hostile local warriors or the frequent mutinies among his own men, all of which were quashed ruthlessly, resulting in numerous executions. Beltrán de Guzmán's tactics earned him an infamous reputation. He plundered villages, destroyed crops, burned dwellings and looted and tortured *caciques* so they'd hand over their riches – if they had any. The Mexican historian Vicente Riva Palacio (1832–96) called him 'the most depraved man who ever walked the soil of Nueva España'.

As Beltrán de Guzmán advanced, sowing death and desolation, he harboured a dream. He wanted to found a city and name it Guadalajara after the Spanish town of his birth. Perhaps he felt nostalgia for his homeland; certainly

no one in Spain missed him. When he reached a place called Nochistlán, he decided to give it a go. He brought in sixty-three settler families and rein-vented himself as an urban planner. It was a disaster. There was scarcely any water, the land was so dry and the soil so hard that it ruined their tools, the local Indige-nous people retaliated with force and the losses were continuous. He suffered the ultimate blow to his pride when one of his lieutenants, Captain Juan de Oñate, founded his own town of Guadalajara. After seeking out a more hospitable area, on 14 February 1542 the lieutenant laid the foundations of the first building (today it is the site of the sumptuous Degol-lado Theatre) in the centre of the Valle de Atemajac. At 1,500 metres above sea level the climate is perfect. It always feels like spring, with clear skies and dry air. Water was abundant thanks to the presence of a nearby river, which was renamed San Juan de Dios and eventually rerouted under the Calzada Independencia in 1909. Beltrán de Guzmán, meanwhile, was conducted back to Spain after a storm of accusations and complaints from both clergymen and settlers, ending his days in misery in the fortress at Torrejón de Velasco. He died in 1544 without ever seeing a single stone of what Mexicans would, over the centuries, transform into la Perla de Occidente, the Pearl of the West.

A very wealthy city, Guadalajara is also culturally vibrant and home to several renowned musicians, not least the group Maná and the extremely popular Vicente Fernández, 'El Rey' of ranchera music. Those from towns nearby include Carlos

Santana (Autlán) and Consuelo Velázquez (Ciudad Guzmán). While Velázquez's name may not be immediately recognisable, he is famous for composing 'Besame Mucho', one of the all-time classic songs. In terms of literature, Guadalajara nurtured Juan Rulfo, one of the finest Mexican writers of the 20th century (no offence to Octavio Paz or Carlos Fuentes). And then there's Luis Barragán, the pride of the capital of Jalisco and the first Latin American to be awarded the Pritzker Prize, one of the top international awards given to architects. After graduating from university, Barragán went on to build most of his modernist houses in Mexico City, with his home/studio eventually declared a UNESCO World Heritage Site.

Guadalajara has expanded dramatically over the years. While the semi-pedestrianised historic centre is an oasis of quiet, stately buildings, churches and squares built in a wide range of styles – from majestic to delicate, from Churrigueresque baroque typical of the colonial period to 19th-century neoclassical to early-20th-century art deco, heavily patrolled by policemen on bicycles – the rest of the city is made up of eight-lane boulevards heaving with traffic, confounding tourists searching for their own imagined Mexico. And yet Guadalajara is a city of *mexicanidad* par excellence. The state of Jalisco, with its mariachi players and skilled *charros* (rodeo riders), is home to the most famous dance troupes and deeply rooted traditions. Everything, in other words, that *extranjeros* consider 'Mexican folklore'.

But Guadalajara has so much more than this. For example, its prestigious university, founded in 1792, now has 300,000 students. There's the Expo, where some of the most important fairs in Latin America are held – notably the International Book Fair (FIL). Inaugurated in 1987, the FIL is second in importance globally only to the Frankfurt Book Fair in terms of business generated and the biggest in the Americas. There's fine dining and nightlife, with countless exquisite restaurants and nightclubs – many designed by famous architects – and numerous museums. In fact, in terms of art, it would be remiss not to mention that Guadalajara was also home to José Clemente Orozco, one of Mexico's greatest muralists (alongside Diego Rivera and David Alfaro Siqueiros), with his frescos adorning some of the city's finest buildings. One such edifice that visitors absolutely shouldn't miss is the Instituto Cultural Cabañas. This architectural complex, which was founded in 1801, took nearly half a century to build

The blue agave plant, from which 100 per cent agave tequila is produced.

The cathedral and its square are two of the most emblematic landmarks in the historic centre of Guadalajara.

and contains no fewer than twenty-three courtyards. It has numerous art, music and dance schools, a theatre, offices and, of course, restaurants. In the central courtyard stands the cruciform chapel known as the Capilla Tolsá, the vaults of which were frescoed by Orozco between 1936 and 1939, a masterpiece of modern art. Among the fifty-three panels is *Man of Fire*, an impressive allegory about the struggle of human beings to free themselves from the yoke of colonialism, with the conquistadors portrayed as the Horsemen of the Apocalypse. This touch of satire speaks to the artist's deep disillusion with the 'men of providence' and the subsequent revolutions, which were inevitably won by the powerful 'leopards' of the day.

Not far from the Cabañas is what is generally considered the largest covered market in the Americas: two vast, crowded floors of market space. Officially it is called Mercado Libertad, but people refer to it familiarly as San Juan de Dios. With its explosion of intoxicating colours and smells, it's easy to temporarily put to the back of your mind the monumental and often austere city and sink down into its more genuine soul. After all, to truly know the places and peoples of Mexico, you have to visit the markets and *cantinas*. There's an abundance of *artesanías* at the market, notably those who work with terracotta – but to truly admire the master potters at work it's best to travel the few kilometres to nearby Tlaquepaque. This small city is the regional capital of ceramics and is a must-see destination for anyone interested in buying ceramics and terracotta handicrafts. Its name comes from the Náhuatl word *tlalipac*, meaning 'mountain of clay'. If you go, one of the key places to visit is El Refugio Cultural Centre, a cluster of buildings originally run as a hospital by nuns. It was restored in 1983 and now serves as a venue for cultural and academic events, hosting both temporary and permanent exhibitions. One part of the complex is home to Pantaleón Panduro Museum, named after the most distinguished earthenware craftsman and founder of the workshop that made the city of Tlaquepaque famous not just in Mexico but across the world. Because the museum also contains numerous pieces from other Mexican states, it offers an unrivalled overview of local ceramics production.

At the town's centre lies El Parián, a large, flower-filled space surrounded by restaurants and *cantinas*: the '*cantina más grande del mundo*'. Here you can enjoy performances by mariachi bands while sitting comfortably in *equipales*, the wood-and-leather armchairs built to designs that pre-date the conquest.

Back in the historic centre of Guadalajara, while walking around and breathing in the 'perfect' climate that beguiled Captain Oñate, one will find additional murals by Orozco at the Palacio de Gobierno de Jalisco. These celebrate the epic story of Father Hidalgo, a priest and leader of the independence movement who issued a decree abolishing slavery in 1810. This historical event is one of many sources of pride for the *tapatíos,* as the inhabitants of Guadalajara and the state of Jalisco are called. The word means 'worth three' and derives from *tapatiotl*, the Náhuatl word for the traditional pouch used to carry cocoa beans when they were used as currency. Even though today's Perla de Occidente is a vast metropolitan area with several neighbouring municipalities and home to close on four million *tapatíos* (and their cars), it hasn't lost

NARCOS: GUADALAJARA

The Guadalajara Cartel was founded in the early 1980s by Miguel Ángel Félix Gallardo, originally from Sinaloa, the territory later dominated by Joaquín 'El Chapo' Guzmán. Gallardo, a former officer in the Federal Police, organised the most powerful cartel in Guadalajara, successfully creating a network among the various territories through which Colombian cocaine travels to the USA. His rise was supported by the corrupt leaders of the now defunct Dirección Federal de Seguridad and bolstered by the CIA, which used him to supply weapons and funds to the Contra mercenaries fighting against Nicaragua's leftist Sandinista government. Gallardo made Guadalajara an oasis of *pax armata* – until he made a fatal error in 1985. Having uncovered a DEA infiltrator, an undercover agent of Mexican extraction named Enrique Camarena, he had him murdered. The DEA plotted its revenge. With the support of local and national politicians, Gallardo managed to keep control until 1989, when he was finally arrested. The series *Narcos: Mexico*, in which Gallardo is played by Diego Luna, one of Mexico's most highly respected actors, was inspired by his story and that of the Guadalajara Cartel. After his fall, the Sinaloa Cartel initially gained the upper hand in Guadalajara under its new boss, Ismael 'El Mayo' Zambada, El Chapo's former right-hand man, but this supremacy was challenged by a new organisation, the Jalisco New Generation Cartel, leading to bloody clashes. Guadalajara's enviable reputation as one of the country's most peaceful cities has suffered heavy blows, even though the violence has declined in recent years. (P.C.)

its charm, no doubt thanks to its genial atmosphere, particularly in the evening when the pace slows down. What the city has lost – and is struggling to restore – is its proud record as a safe metropolis. Sadly, with all the money in circulation, it has attracted narco traffickers, who often settle their scores on the city's streets.

Not far from the town of Tequila is the cellar of producer Las Tres Mujeres, where the spirit continues its ageing in casks.

*

Among the many museums in Guadalajara, that dedicated to the army and air force and, more particularly, to Mexico's contribution to the Second World War, attracts few tourists but a good number of Mexicans keen on learning about their history. There's even a P-47 Thunderbolt fighter that was part of Escuadrón 201, the squadron that fought against the Japanese in the Philippines. Although Mexico was reluctant to become involved in the conflict, the Germans provoked them to such a degree – torpedoing and sinking the oil tankers that kept the Allied countries supplied – that President Manuel Ávila Camacho was forced to ask parliament to declare war on the Axis powers. Two very particular things came out of this. First, it gave the Mexicans the excuse to requisition and nationalise the vast holdings in the Chiapas region that belonged to the family of Eva Braun, Hitler's companion and later wife, which were made up of extensive coffee plantations where Indigenous peoples were treated as slaves. Second, it allowed Mexico to impound ten Italian merchant ships that were anchored in Veracruz and Tampico – the only occasion that Mexico had to 'capture' any enemy combatants. The Italian crews, made up of about four hundred sailors, primarily from Liguria, were 'deported' to Guadalajara – perhaps to distance them from the sea and minimise their chances of escaping. Whatever the reason, the sailors were not imprisoned, rather they were allowed to roam freely, and no one treated them like prisoners, much less as enemies. In fact, once the war was over most of them remained in Guadalajara, married Mexican women and had children, leading to a curious mini colony of Ligurians in the heart of Jalisco.

Perhaps more than any other city in Mexico, Guadalajara is a store of deep Mexican traditions. The *cantina* is both its symbol and an endless source of inspiration for any travel writer making their way through the land. For Mexicans the *cantina* is not merely a bar where they drink and eat *botanas* – the free snacks that help customers soak up as much alcohol as possible – the *cantina* is a sacred place, a temple of unity, safe from the

There's no shortage of endorsements from American VIPs. Tequila is no longer just a drink enjoyed by young people in tequila slammers. It is now associated with luxurious lifestyles as well as a lucrative investment, as George Clooney has demonstrated. Casamigos, the brand founded by the actor with two partners in 2013 and sold on just four years later for a billion dollars, saw its value increase by more than any other brand in the alcoholic drinks sector in the following five years. In the decade to 2022 tequila exports grew from $849 million in 2012 to almost $4 billion. In tandem with the tequila boom, the market for mezcal has also taken off in recent years. Until recently mezcal was seen as tequila's little brother, smokier and more underground – and it is precisely this whiff of authenticity on which to hang a 'craft' label that explains the success of the drink, which, in truth, is the father of all agave spirits while tequila is only the 'blue' variant from the state of Jalisco. Mezcal is made from over thirty types of agave, and in Mexican culture it has a ritual value associated with the celebration of feasts and festivals. The family-business and semi-clandestine nature of the complex traditional methods of distillation makes it difficult for producers to obtain a Denominación de Origen stamp, and many are forced to use the less prestigious 'agave spirit' on their products. Rather than an example to follow, the rise of tequila seems more of a warning: sky-high agave prices have small producers on the ropes, and there is a risk that biodiversity will give way to more profitable monocultures while production ends up in just a few hands.

wearying rhythms of the city. It's somewhere a person can pass their afternoons and evenings playing dominoes – the quintessential game of any true *cantina*. It's the ideal place to meet and do business in a more relaxed manner than in a sterile office. In a *cantina* customers can sing along with the mariachis, and if you're in the mood for getting drunk you can be sure someone will keep you company without passing judgement. And, on the off-chance things get out of hand, there are always the *meseros*, the shrewd *cantineros* who know how to defuse a fight before anything gets too serious. Even so, visitors will still need to learn how to *agarrar la onda*, a ubiquitous phrase in Mexico that means something like 'take a hint' or 'play the game' and never force a situation. Guadalajara rivals Mexico City in the number of its *cantinas*, with the most famous undoubtedly La Fuente. Founded in 1921, it's also known as 'the one with the bicycle' after the bike that a drunk patron apparently placed on top of a column under a stone archway back in 1957. What makes the story legendary is that the man didn't actually come in to the *cantina* with a bike but somehow he managed to use it to pay his bill, as a kind of pledge. If you ask the heirs of the founder, they'll tell you that it was the *cantinero* who hoisted it far up above the heads of his customers so that the debtor would see it clearly when he came back – which, of course, he never did. Consequently, it's also the oldest (and grimiest) bicycle in Guadalajara, protected by layers of dust and grease from the *fritangas* that keep the rust at bay.

Here in Guadalajara and across Jalisco tequila is the main source of export revenue. You can even take a train tour on the Tequila Express from the centre of Guadalajara to all the places where the drink is traditionally produced. Tequila is not only the name of the valley where Mexico's iconic liquor has been made for centuries it's also the name of the town where the distilleries are located. The word itself comes from the Náhuatl *téquitl*, which means 'work' or 'craft', and while it might be hard for most of us to put tequila and work in the same bracket, in Mexico it refers to the specific task of cutting the agave leaves to obtain the sugar-rich juice, or *aguamiel*. The word *tequio*, meanwhile, refers to the farmer. For whatever mysterious reason, Mother Nature seems to have decided that the agave for tequila, a variety known as *azul* or Weber Azul, grows and thrives only here in this little corner of Mexico. All attempts to transplant it – notably efforts made by the Americans and Japanese – have failed. Even in neighbouring Mexican states, where other varieties proliferate, this one does not, thanks to a complex microclimate and a particular balance between soil, water, climate, altitude and so on. Indeed, when you consider just how easy it is to find a bottle labelled as tequila, you have to wonder if it actually contains the genuine distillate; all the plantations in Jalisco could never produce the amount of the spirit on sale worldwide. While Mexican law is very strict in

this regard, people outside the country don't realise that when a label simply states 'tequila', it means that it is a *mixto*, that 51 per cent is agave alcohol and 49 per cent is cane alcohol, so when you buy tequila you're only drinking 'half' aguardiente. When the label says '100 per cent agave', then it's tequila, and if it says '100 per cent agave azul', better still. But even the big distilleries have lowered their standards to meet customer demand, so if you want to taste real tequila you'll have to travel all the way to Mexico and visit the small family-run businesses with their limited production and unknown labels, most of which are impossible to obtain elsewhere.

Although the Tren Tapatío – which, with its luxurious sleeping cars and busy *cantina*, used to make its sedate way from Mexico City to the capital of Jalisco – is sadly no more, these days Guadalajara is served by excellent highways, which allow visitors to get to all the must-see destinations. First among these is Lake Chapala, the largest body of water in Mexico, and then, of course, there is the Pacific coast, with Puerto Vallarta a major destination both for domestic and foreign tourists. Situated in the middle of the broad Bahía de Banderas and surrounded by small towns that were once quiet fishing villages, including La Cruz de Huanacaxtle – named after the majestic century-old tree that stands at the entrance to the pueblo – Puerto Vallarta is located in the heart of the state of Nayarit, just across the Río Ameca. It became famous in the mid-1960s after the director John Huston chose it as a location for his film version of Tennessee Williams's novel *The Night of the Iguana*. It is where the rocky love story between Richard Burton and Liz Taylor began, with the diva also falling in love with the place and building

A display of cowboy boots at the Mercado San Juan de Dios in central Guadalajara; these boots are very popular in the area as well as in northern Mexico.

'John Huston regretted the attention he brought to Puerto Vallarta, as it led to the arrival of packs of rowdy Americans, whom he resented.'

a mansion there. Ava Gardner, meanwhile, managed to create such a stir when she was in town that the paparazzi flocked to Puerto Vallarta, turning what had been a sleepy, unknown village into a hotspot and sealing its fate. Huston stayed on long afterwards, and many a signed photo hangs on the walls of the *cantinas* downtown – there's even a square named after him, complete with a bronze statue. He regretted the attention he brought to the town, as it led to the arrival of packs of rowdy Americans, whom he resented.

Visitors seeking peace and quiet travel to Yelapa, a sandy cove nestling in the mountains just a little further south and easily accessible by sea. While there is a narrow road that winds up and through the Sierras from Vallarta to Yelapa, complete with hairpin bends and lots of dust (or mud, depending on the season), it is much quicker and easier to get there by water. Boats set sail from the pier at Playa de los Muertos, named for the cemetery that was there long before Huston & Co. arrived. Perhaps to make up for this rather forbidding name, the local authorities called the surrounding neighbourhood Zona Romántica, and today it is filled with restaurants and bars where people gather to watch the sunset.

I travelled to Yelapa around twenty years ago. Back then the area didn't have mains electricity, and the fridges in the little beach restaurants were powered by portable generators. I met Indigenous people as well as foreigners, some of whom had been there a very long time, people who wanted nothing more than to live simply and breathe clean air. The village had water thanks to a strange tangle of rubber hoses that made their way down the verdant mountain. When we traced them uphill we came upon a waterfall and a 'parking lot' full of mules and horses, which were the only means of transportation besides boats in this roadless village.

I asked a local girl if she thought things would always stay this way. She said she imagined that one day they'd have electricity but never a road. 'No one wants a road! We want to keep Yelapa as it is. Sure, it's true, we're only a few hours away from one of Mexico's busiest tourist centres, but the people who come here want total peace and quiet. A road would bring cars, buses, pollution ... No thank you!' Commendable, I thought. Then she smiled mischievously and added, 'I should also mention that there's more marijuana in these mountains than there are palm trees. It's a major source of income locally. So, we're better off without crowds ...' Ah well, that explains it.

Today Yelapa is a charming little town with murals and mosaics, only a short distance from the metropolis of Puerto Vallarta and the millions of tourists who flock to the Bahía de Banderas each year. Despite the presence of tourists, the soul of Mexico still exists. It's visible in a thousand small details of everyday life, in feasts and festivals, in well-known markets and smaller ones. Even people who travel here for their all-inclusive beach vacations want to experience it. In this great country, with its rich identity and deep roots, *mexicanidad* continues to permeate every single aspect of life. ✒

Frida Kahlo and the Birth of Fridolatry

Witch, savage, icon, Barbie: the legend of Frida Kahlo is one of colonial narratives and grotesque commercial exploitation.

VALERIA LUISELLI

A poster of Frida Kahlo on sale at the shop in the museum devoted to the artist in Mexico City.

Frida, the unapologetic bitch. Frida, the disabled artist. Frida, symbol of radical feminism. Frida, the victim of Diego. Frida, the chic, gender-fluid, beautiful and monstrous icon. Frida tote bags, Frida keychains, Frida T-shirts and also 2018's Frida Barbie doll (no unibrow). Frida Kahlo has been subject to global scrutiny and commercial exploitation. She has been appropriated by curators, historians, artists, actors, activists, Mexican consulates, museums and Madonna.

Over the years this avalanche has trivialised Kahlo's work to fit a shallow 'Fridolatry'. And, while some criticism has been able to counter the views that cast her as a naive, infantile, almost involuntary artist, most narratives have continued to position her as a geographically marginal painter: one more developing-world artist waiting to be 'discovered', one more voiceless subject waiting to be 'translated'.

In 1938 Frida Kahlo painted *Lo que el agua me dio* (*What the Water Gave Me*), the painting perhaps responsible for launching her international career but also her international mistranslation. In this self-portrait of sorts, we see Kahlo's feet and calves inside a bathtub and, above them, as if emanating from the steam, a collaged landscape: an erupting volcano out of which a skyscraper emerges; a dead bird resting on a tree; a strangled woman; a Tehuana dress dramatically spread out; a female couple resting on a floating cork. Kahlo was working on *Lo que el agua me dio* when the French surrealist André Breton arrived in Mexico for a visit. He was transfixed by it. He called Kahlo a 'natural surrealist', and in a brochure endorsing her New York debut at Julien Levy's gallery in 1938, he wrote: 'My surprise and joy were unbounded when I discovered, on my arrival in Mexico, that her work has blossomed forth, in her latest paintings, into pure surreality, despite the fact that it had been conceived without any prior knowledge whatsoever of the ideas motivating the activities of my friends and myself.'

Although 'natural surrealist' was a label that helped translate Kahlo's paintings for European and American audiences, it was one that she always rejected.

VALERIA LUISELLI is an acclaimed writer of both fiction and non-fiction. She is the author of *Sidewalks*, *Faces in the Crowd*, *The Story of My Teeth*, *Tell Me How It Ends* and *Lost Children Archive*. She is the recipient of a 2019 MacArthur Fellowship and the winner of DUBLIN Literary Award, two *Los Angeles Times* Book Prizes, the Carnegie Medal and an American Book Award and has been nominated for the National Book Critics Circle Award, the Kirkus Prize and the Booker Prize. Her work has appeared in *The New Yorker*, *The New York Times*, *Granta* and *McSweeney's*, among other publications, and has been translated into more than twenty languages. She teaches at Bard College, New York, and is a visiting professor at Harvard University.

To be projected as a 'surrealist' in Europe helped audiences to understand her work more immediately – more palatably. She was branded as authentically Mexican, with international flair. But to be seen as a '*natural* surrealist' also transformed her into a kind of *sauvage*: unconscious of her talent, unsuspecting of her mastery. After her debut a *Time* magazine critic described her work as having 'the daintiness of miniatures, the vivid reds and yellows of Mexican tradition and the playfully bloody fancy of an unsentimental child'.

Kahlo was hardly unsuspecting, hardly unconscious of what she was doing and who she was. She knew how to capitalise on the elements of her private life and cultural heritage, curate them carefully and use them to build her public persona. She was a mestiza, born in Mexico City, who had adopted a traditional Zapotec-Tehuana 'look'. Her father, the German-born Carl Wilhelm 'Guillermo' Kahlo, was a well-known photographer, and the family lived in a neocolonial mansion in Coyoacán, the famous Casa Azul. Kahlo was very much aware of the complex politics of selfhood she was creating and manipulating. In a 1939 photograph, taken during the opening of Kahlo's first exhibition in Paris, she is posing in front of *Lo que el agua me dio*. She is wearing a Tehuana dress, and her unibrow is underscored with black eyeliner: Frida representing Frida. (It is unclear which one is the artwork.)

The way Kahlo's work and persona were read in Mexico was, of course, very different from the way they were translated into other cultural milieux. Just as Breton had attached the category 'natural surrealist' to her art and framed her work in a discourse that she herself did not embrace, many others did the same with various aspects of her public and private life.

An interesting example of this is the house and studio in Mexico City where she and Diego Rivera lived and worked during some of their most productive years in the 1930s. It was designed by Juan O'Gorman, the young architect who was then pioneering the radical architectural changes that took place in post-revolutionary Mexico City.

Before the Mexican Revolution (1910–20) 19th-century neoclassical and colonial architecture dominated. French-influenced mansions across the city stood like lonely homages to a quickly decaying European noble class, and the family life of the Mexican bourgeoisie played out in the sumptuous and darkened stages of these interiors, with their heavy drapes and excessive ornamentation. But after the Revolution new ideas about hygiene, ventilation, comfort, efficiency and simplicity made their way into the city. Houses, and with them daily life, were transformed radically and rapidly.

Frida Kahlo's work *Lo que el agua me dio* (Paris, Daniel Filipacchi Collection).

'The house was an emblem of modernity and a kind of manifesto: a solitary example of a new functionalism in a city that was still trying to find a national architectural language that best suited its revolutionary programme.'

Attuned to the ideological and architectural changes taking place, the couple asked O'Gorman to design a studio and house for them. He created a space specifically for a couple of painters – at once separated and connected. The buildings were the first in Mexico designed for specific functional requirements: living, painting and showcasing work.

In 1933, a few years after Kahlo and Rivera married, they moved in. Rivera's area was larger, with more work space. Kahlo's was more 'homely', with a studio that could transform into a bedroom. A flight of stairs led from her studio to a rooftop, which was connected by a bridge to Rivera's space. Beyond being a workplace, it became a space for the couple's extramarital affairs: Rivera with his models and secretaries; Kahlo with certain talented and famous men, from the sculptor and designer Isamu Noguchi to Leon Trotsky. Perhaps without knowing it, O'Gorman designed a house whose function it was to allow an 'open' relationship.

The house was an emblem of modernity and a kind of manifesto: a solitary example of a new functionalism in a city that was still trying to find a national architectural language that best suited its revolutionary programme. It did not encode traditional values or messages. It simply addressed the practical necessities of its dwellers, was materially efficient (primarily made of reinforced concrete), socially progressive and cheap.

With time, however, as neutral as the buildings may have been intended to be in their architecture, they ended up functioning as a site of Mexican cultural capital, especially one connected to indigenous Mexican craftsmanship. The couple were hosts to visitors who came to see their work and works-in-progress, as well as their collections of arts and crafts: Trotsky, Nelson Rockefeller, Pablo Neruda, John Dos Passos, Sergei Eisenstein, Breton.

O'Gorman gave Rivera and Kahlo a machine to live in, as Le Corbusier would have had it, but also a machine to translate in. Their home brought in foreignness as much as it served as a platform to project a particular idea of Mexico to the world. More than anything it provided the stage for the power couple of Mexican modernity: cosmopolitan, sophisticated, well connected and more Mexican than Mexico. The couple's ultimate oeuvre was, of course, themselves. Kahlo and Rivera were, perhaps, Mexico's first performance artists, and their *casa-estudio* was their very own gallery.

In 1934 the photographer Martin Munkácsi visited Mexico and copiously

The entrance to one of the rooms in the Frida Kahlo Museum, also known as the Casa Azul.

documented the house and studios. The pictures had been commissioned for *Harper's Bazaar*, the New York-based fashion magazine which was directed at an upper-class female audience, mostly American but also French and British. In *Harper's* July 1934 issue, a double-page spread titled 'Colors of Mexico' displayed three of Munkácsi's many photographs: one of Kahlo crossing the bridge from one house to the other; one of Rivera working in his studio; and one of Frida climbing the staircase to the roof. In the centre of the layout there is a large photograph of the couple walking beside the cactus fence; a caption explains 'Diego Rivera with Señora Freida [*sic*] Kahlo de Rivera before the cactus fence of their Mexico City home'.

The buildings were designed to embody a *proletkult* ideology, resembling a factory or industrial complex, with its visible water tanks, its exposed materials and raised supporting columns. The cactus fence surrounding the house, if seen in relation to it, added to the general industrial feeling. However, *Harper's* chose the image that best *decontextualised* the cactus fence and thus presented it as a folkloric, decorative element. To the right of that central image appeared a series of photographs of barefooted Mexican peasants selling crafts and riding mules.

An accompanying piece written by Harry Block – a New York editor – describes his search for the perfect Mexican sandals: 'All Mexico walks on *huaraches* (pronounced wahratchehs and meaning sandals) ...' Juxtaposed with the portrait of Rivera and Kahlo – he, dressed like a European dandy, solid leather shoes included; she, wearing pointy black boots – Block's ode to the *huarache* seems rather forced.

At the entrance to the Frida Kahlo Museum a street vendor offers souvenirs inspired by the Mexican artist. In the space of a few years the museum has become the second most visited in Mexico City.

HOW NOT TO BUILD A MEGACITY

It would perhaps be unfair, just this once, to pin the blame on Cortés, but building Mexico City on an unstable crust of clay and volcanic rock was not such a smart idea, and now that the capital has become a megacity of more than twenty million people it is paying the price for a series of bad decisions. The Spanish destroyed the island city of Tenochtitlan and built another in the European style, draining the lake that surrounded it and embarking on a never-ending war against the seasonal rains that filled the depression as if it were a bowl. (In the 17th century, after a particularly violent flood, the city remained under water for five years.) Reclamation of the former lake and the construction of drainage channels – the *Desagüe* – was completed after independence, and it is one of the most ambitious hydraulic-engineering projects in human history. But then, in the mid-20th century, the city began to grow rapidly. Aqueducts were constructed to bring water from neighbouring areas and so guarantee supply, and then more were built to ever more distant regions (today it is estimated that 40 per cent of the water is lost in transit over such long distances) and use of the groundwater beneath the city was intensified. However, rapid urbanisation, and the (understandable) obsession with pumping away rainwater as soon as possible to avoid floods, prevents the groundwater from replenishing, causing continual water crises while the city sinks into the void left behind by the water that has been pumped out – in some areas dropping up to half a metre a year. The effects can be seen in the uneven, broken paving of its streets and the floors of its buildings. Another way that Moctezuma has found to take his revenge.

'More than anything their *casa-estudio* provided the stage for the power couple of Mexican modernity: cosmopolitan, sophisticated, well connected and more Mexican than Mexico.'

The *Harper's* piece is a perfect example of how Mexico was perpetuated in such stories as a marginal space, with glimpses of modernity a rare exception to the rule. The magazine shows an utterly foreign Mexico, but in a way that also makes it easier to capture and explain to foreign audiences through its associated clichés.

A mural of Frida Kahlo wearing a mask at Constituyentes metro station in Mexico City.

It is a form of translation that simplifies the complex operations that took place in the Rivera-Kahlo home.

A functionalist Mexican house that showcased post-revolutionary art? Impossible! Let's just use the picture with the cacti.

This instance of colonising narratives in cultural translations was not the end but the beginning. In 2002 Harvey Weinstein's company distributed the film *Frida*, starring Salma Hayek, asked for a more sexy Kahlo – more nudity, less unibrow – and got away with it. In a 2016 concert stunt in Mexico, Madonna pulled a Frida lookalike from the audience, said she was 'so excited' to finally meet Frida and then handed her a banana as a token.

Last Halloween my 21-year-old niece was dragged by her friend to a New York college party. She wasn't wearing a costume, was not really in the mood. At some point a trio of Wonder Women stumbled in: red knee-high boots, star-print bikini bottoms, strapless tops, gold headbands fastened around long blonde hair.

One of the three wonders took a long swig from a bottle and almost fell back, suddenly noticing my niece standing behind her. She turned around and looked straight into her face. She studied it up close. Like many women in my maternal family, my niece inherited a dark, robust unibrow. The Wonder Woman finally said, 'Oh my God, it's Frida Kahlo!' 🐦

La Curandera

IVAN CAROZZI

Translated by Oonagh Stransky

H anging on the wall of the Guggen-heim Museum in New York City between May and September 2022 was a painting of a petite woman dressed in a traditional Central American *huipil* embroidered with colourful flowers. Painted by Cecilia Vicuña, two-time winner of the Venice Biennale Golden Lion, the work pays tribute to Maria Sabina Magdalena García, better known as Maria Sabina. Although Maria Sabina lived her entire life (1894–1985) in Huautla de Jiménez, a small town in the Sierra Maza-teca in the Mexican state of Oaxaca, and never once left the mountains, in the 1960s she became a deeply venerated figure for the counterculture and a frequent subject of study by people interested in psyche-delics, anthropology and altered states of consciousness.

Born into a humble farming family, Maria Sabina was a *curandera*, or shaman, and heir to the ancient religious prac-tice based on the therapeutic use of

IVAN CAROZZI is an Italian author and TV writer, whose credits include *Le invasioni barbari-che*, *Lessico famigliare* and *Dilemmi*. He was editor-in-chief of *Linus* magazine and writes for a number of publications, such as *Il Post*, *Il Tascabile*, *cheFare* and *minima&moralia*. He is the author of *Macao* (2012), *I figli delle stelle* (2014), *Teneri violenti* (2016), *L'età della tigre* (2019) and in 2022 published his essay on the future of work *Fine lavoro mai*.

hallucinogenic mushrooms known as *teonanácatl*. The great wealth and variety of hallucinogenic mushrooms and plants that can be found in Mexico, not least the famous peyote, goes a long way to explain the country's magical and visionary mindset – a perspective that has survived despite the prohibitions imposed on the people by Spanish rule – and one that still influences art and culture.

Maria Sabina shot to fame in 1957 after an article entitled 'Seeking the Magic Mushroom' was published in the American weekly magazine *Life*. The author of the piece, Robert Gordon Wasson, was a banker and self-taught ethnomycologist. He and his Russian-American wife, Valentina Pavlovna, had been studying mushrooms for a long time and were especially keen to understand the role that fungi have played in the evolution of human culture. According to Wasson and Pavlovna, the visions that came from the psychoactive properties of certain fungi when used by certain civilisations were responsible for the emergence of a unique relationship with the divine, consequently giving rise to cults and various religious traditions. In June 1955 Wasson travelled to the Sierra Mazateca with photographer Allan Richardson. The two men made their way up to Huautla de Jiménez, at an altitude of 1,600 metres above sea level, to take part in a ceremony at which Maria Sabina was to officiate. Wasson, who described the shaman as petite and 'with a spirituality in her expression', had asked to participate in a *velada*, a ritual that relied not only on the consumption of *Psilocybe caerulescens* – a mushroom containing the alkaloid known as psilocybin – but also involved songs and litanies as well as the use of candles. In Wasson's conversation with her he specifically asked about *'nti sheeto*, carefully articulating the word – complete with the glottal stop and tonal differentiation – for the sacred mushroom in the local Mixtec dialect. The encounter with Maria Sabina was of great historical and anthropological importance; there had never been a record or chronicle of a white man taking part in a *velada*. Within half an hour of taking the mushrooms Richardson informed Wasson that he was starting to have visions. Wasson tried to calm Richardson while also confessing that he, too, was having his first hallucinations. Wasson compared his visions to the traditional decorations seen on carpets and textiles. Later that night, while Maria Sabina sang to them, he had visions of courtyards, gardens and palaces covered with precious stones. He also said that the walls of the room dissolved, allowing him to float freely in mid-air and take in the views of vast mountainous landscapes that were traversed by camel trains.

In among the advertisements for Whirlpool refrigerators and Ford convertibles, the photo reportage that appeared in *Life* explained the different stages of the ceremony and offered its readers, who were hungry for exoticism, an exceptionally valuable historical document. Not only were readers transported to a place that was entirely foreign to 'normal' America in the 1950s and located somewhere in mysterious Mexico but they were propelled on a journey through time by the careful description of this ancestral rite, the roots of which might date back to pre-Columbian times. Robert Gordon Wasson, dressed in a trench coat and armed with a notebook, was immortalised in a photograph taken before the ritual began as he jotted down some notes while the slight figure of Maria Sabina carefully arranged some mushrooms on plates. Another photo captures a moment when the mushrooms are having their effect: Maria

Sabina reaching over the reclining body of a young woman, as if assisting her in a moment of particular euphoria and excitement triggered by the *Psilocybe caerulescens*. The photos show that the ceremony takes place in the *curandera*'s humble home; there are traditional mats spread out on the floor and an altar formed by a crucifix and a pair of framed prints with a religious theme. Maria Sabina's chants were recorded by Wasson and then put out as an LP by Folkways Records under the title *Mushroom Ceremony of the Mazatec Indians of Mexico*. The recording is still available today. Maria's hallucinations inspired the words to her songs; she sang in Mixtec, as she didn't know Spanish and was illiterate. Thanks in part to the dissemination of the recordings, Maria Sabina came to be considered a poet. Her lyrics have been translated into Spanish and English and are much appreciated by poets such as Anne Waldman.

It is thanks to this article in *Life* that the American public learned about Maria Sabina and the remote village of Huautla de Jiménez. Soon the town became a key destination for scientists and anthropologists, and such a popular pilgrimage for hippies that the streets of Huautla and other nearby villages were filled with Westerners on mushrooms, often without following any sort of ritual. Legend has it that even John Lennon and Bob Dylan once came looking for Maria Sabina. The resulting bustle, however, prompted the Mexican authorities to intervene, and Maria Sabina came to be considered something of a drug dealer, and the constant flow of tourists created such a disturbance to the peace that some of the Indigenous people turned against the shaman and ostracised her. Maria Sabina died in poverty at the age of ninety-one. As a young girl she had learned how to care for goats and chickens, plant corn, knead and bake tortillas, sew, wash and sweep her yard. If the stories that come down to us about her life are true, she started taking mushrooms around the age of seven, circa 1901, when she went to look for one of her animals that had escaped. Apparently she came across the mushrooms and ate them because she was hungry.

The wave of Westerners that made their way to Huautla de Jiménez because of the legend of Maria Sabina is a classic example of 'spiritual tourism' blending with 'psychedelic tourism', a phenomenon that has become ever more common. It occurs not only in Mexico but in other regions of Central and South America where people can take part in ancient shamanic practices using psychedelic substances obtained from plants of various kinds, be they mushrooms or an ayahuasca infusion (teas brewed from plants with hallucinogenic properties). Naturally, shamanic traditions have been impacted by these changes; ancient rituals have become contaminated with New Age elements, traditional shamans have vanished and

shrewd figures only interested in making money now oversee the practices. A place where this happens frequently is San José del Pacifico, which, at 2,600 meters above sea level in the Oaxaca region, is only a few hours' drive from the beaches of Zipolite and Puerto Escondido. Visitors can take in the stunning views, go on amazing hikes in the woods and even experience a *temazcal*, a sweat lodge (or 'house of heat' as it is known in Náhuatl). Naturally there's also an abundance of hallucinogenic mushrooms. In fact, among the houses for rent, there's even a charming one built in the shape of a mushroom, decorated with white dots on a red roof. San José has now become something of a hotspot, and people travel there from all over the world. It's hard to say just how long the poetry of the place will remain with the tourist influx and its fallout.

Nowadays when visitors arrive in Huautla de Jiménez they are greeted by a large arch and the word 'Bienvenido' preceded and followed by images of mushrooms. A little further on there's even a sculpture of a mushroom with the figure of Maria Sabina sitting on top. Maria Sabina's old home – a prefabricated structure given to her in 1979 by the sister of José López Portillo, the president of Mexico at the time – is now a small museum where *huipils* and gifts once brought to her are on view. Although the use and sale of hallucinogenic mushrooms remains illegal in Mexico, in recent years parliament has had to consider many petitions in their favour; some ask for legalisation, others ask for the therapeutic virtues of psilocybin to be recognised, others claim that hallucinogenic mushrooms should be honoured for their biocultural heritage. The figure of Maria Sabina as a simple peasant woman and shaman has been the focus of documentaries, books and numerous scientific articles. She has been written about by scholars of art, anthropology, psychoanalysis and cultural studies. And, as exemplified by artist and activist Cecilia Vicuña's painting, *abuelita* Maria Sabina is still considered a symbol of Mexico and Central America and a vital link to the people's ancestral wisdom and culture, much of which was crushed during periods of conquest by Europeans.

An Author Recommends

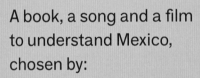

A book, a song and a film to understand Mexico, chosen by:

JAZMINA BARRERA
Translated by Simon Deefholts

Jazmina Barrera is a writer born in Mexico City. Her books have been published in nine countries and translated into English – Two Lines Press issued *On Lighthouses* (2020) and *Linea Nigra: An Essay on Pregnancy and Earthquakes* (2022) and *Cross-Stitch* will be published in late 2023 – Italian, Dutch and French, and her work has also appeared in various print and digital magazines, including *The Paris Review*, *El País*, *Words Without Borders*, *El Malpensante*, *Electric Literature*, *Vice* and *The New York Times*. She is the editor and co-founder of Ediciones Antílope.

THE FILM
TEMPESTAD ('STORM')
Tatiana Huezo
2016

Tempestad traverses Mexico from north to south (in the documentary we see how a storm travels right across the country), from Matamoros to Cancún. On the way we learn about Miriam Carvajal, a woman unjustly imprisoned for people trafficking, and Adela Alvarado, a circus performer who has been searching for her missing daughter for the past ten years. As we listen to their desperate tales the documentary takes us on a bus ride, with images of the realities of Mexican society: poverty, beauty, melancholy, violence. Tatiana Huezo penetrates the country's darkest recesses with a subtlety and attention to detail that make her portrayal all the more devastating. She does, however, find glimmers of light in the darkness: the hopes of two women who (like so many others) choose to resist and try to break the relentless cycle of violence.

THE SONG
CANCIÓN SIN MIEDO
('A Song Without Fear')
Vivir Quintana
2020

THE BOOK
INSTRUCCIONES PARA VIVIR EN MÉXICO
('Instructions on How to Live in Mexico')
Jorge Ibargüengoitia
Editorial Planeta Mexicana, 2019 (Spanish edition)

'What is that song?' I asked my cousin as we were marching on International Women's Day on 8 March. We were dripping with sweat, tired from the sun, happy to be together and occasionally tearful. 'Don't you recognise it? It's by Vivir Quintana,' she tells me and takes out her phone to send me a link. We can hear it from somewhere ahead of us, over to the right:

I'm Claudia, I'm Esther and I'm Teresa
I'm Ingrid, I'm Fabiola and I'm Valeria
I'm the girl you grabbed
I'm the mother who mourns her dead girls
I'm the woman who will make you pay.

Recently I have read reports of feminist marches in Mexico that portray a false image of sisterly harmony. They are not like that. There are the hooded anarchists writing slogans on wall, smashing windows and singing along with Vivir Quintana, 'I'll burn it all down, I'll smash it all up, if you get blinded by some guy one day.' There are the women from the National Action Party, very well turned out, shouting, 'No violence!' There are shouts of 'Men go home!' – and indignant men shouting back – there are radical feminists and trans-inclusive groups. The marches are like the different branches of feminism itself, diverse and complicated, full of tension and disagreement, but there is always common ground – that, for example, we cannot continue to live in a country where eleven women are murdered every day. We can't go on living, that's what it boils down to. And that's what is captured by that song, which has become, along with 'Un violador en tu camino' ('A Rapist in Your Path') by the Chilean group Las Tesis, an anthem for the struggle and a cry of despair.

The book opens with a dinner arranged by a group of Mexicans in honour of a French artist who is visiting Mexico. During the *sobremesa*, when guests relax around the table after a heavy meal – and which in Mexico can last until the next meal is served – someone tells a joke, and the Frenchman, M. Ripois, replies in a mixture of Spanish and French, 'You have a sad history, and yet you've managed to stay happy.' This is a central theme of the work of Jorge Ibargüengoitia, one of the most brilliant writers to have been born on Mexican soil, who discovers humour in each of our national catastrophes. Ibargüengoitia dwells on this ability to find happiness in the face of disaster, most notable in our famous Day of the Dead celebrations. *Instrucciones* ... teaches us, in the form of a manual, about the official history, customs, institutions and absurdities of the country. Nowadays it is clear that the country we call Mexico is a jumble of fictions. There are many more differences than similarities between the individuals who reside between the Río Bravo and the Lacandon Jungle. It is increasingly risky to generalise about a multicultural country, where at least sixty-nine languages are spoken (on a diminishing scale), and yet Ibargüengoitia manages to identify stereotypical attitudes, circumstances, individuals and bureaucratic nightmares that anyone who lives here cannot fail to recognise. Starting with the baroque ritual of personal introductions all the way through to the tragedies of recent years, this book is the best possible introduction to Mexican eccentricities.

The Playlist

You can listen to this playlist at:
open.spotify.com/user/iperborea

RULO DAVID
Translated by Kit Maude

Twelve songs for *The Passenger*, all released in recent years in Mexico and across the world. I've not made any attempt to capture some kind of 'Mexican sound' because that simply isn't possible. There just isn't any one style of music that at this point in the 21st century could possibly represent the Mexican music scene. Just as there are many kinds of Mexican cuisine, all of which are quite distinct from one another, there are many different kinds of Mexican music, and they don't have all that much in common. So I decided to offer an arbitrary and extremely personal selection from a range of genres, all tracks I like very much that seem relevant to the moment and that I'd like the readers of this magazine to listen to as well. Some are well known already – tunes you might hear blaring out as a bus horn in Mexico or songs played over a supermarket PA – others are by lesser-known, more experimental musicians who have appeared on the scene more recently. These include La Bruja de Texcoco – whose voice reminds me of Anohni, another accomplished songwriter – although my choice here reveals the influence of the *corrido tumbado* style (a sub-genre of *corrido*, the traditional ballad

that adopts a hip hop sensibility both musically and in the lyrics, which are often inspired by violence, sex and drug use), and the Sgt. Papers, one of the rockier selections. As elsewhere in the world, rock in Mexico appears to be on its way out.

Over the last couple of years both the pop and traditional music scenes have evolved significantly: hip hop and electronic music have crossed over, and new paths are being forged with fresh, original sounds that appeal to new generations. One example is the collaboration between Los Dos Carnales – a regional Mexican band – and Cartel de Santa, popular veterans of the Mexican hip hop scene. The reverse is also true: more experimental musicians are continuously demonstrating that mainstream music – which these days one might describe as being dominated by the *banda norteña* (contemporary folk with traditional dance rhythms), *corrido* and reggaeton genres – has influenced their work, as seen in 'Cumbia con Jazz' by Grupo Jejeje and 'A Ver Ven Pa'ca' by Suricata. We owe much of this innovation to Café Tacvba, the band that opens the playlist, who since the 1990s have shown an impressive ability to adapt sounds and styles from the past and present, music for the ages, to contemporary tastes, garnering considerable success and acclaim along the way.

RULO DAVID has worked in Mexican radio for over twenty-five years as a DJ, presenter and programmer for a number of stations and hosts one of the most popular radio shows in Mexico, *Poderoso*, on Radio Convoy. He is also a writer, editor and music producer.

1

Café Tacvba
Futuro
2017

2

Juan Cirerol
Metanfeta
2013

3

Silvana
Estrada
Carta
2022

4

Run the Jewels
(feat. Santa Fe Klan)
Ooh La La (Mexican
Institute of Sound Remix)
2022

5

Son Rompe
Pera
*Pájaro
Cenzontle*
2020

6

Suricata
A Ver Ven Pa'ca
2021

7

Silverio
Perro
2013

8

Sgt. Papers
*Échale
Campeón*
2021

9

Cartel de
Santa, Los
dos Carnales
*Aka Entre
el Humo*
2022

10

La Bruja
de Texcoco
*Tiempera de
Granizo*
2022

11

Las
Decapitadas
*Cumbia
Feminista*
2022

12

Grupo Jejeje
*Cumbia
con Jazz*
(Rebajada
Sonido Dueñez)
2020

Digging Deeper

FICTION

Guillermo Arriaga
The Untameable
MacLehose, 2021

Mario Bellatin
Beauty Salon
Deep Vellum, 2021

Roberto Bolaño
2666
Farrar, Straus and Giroux, 2008,
USA / Picador, 2009, UK

Carmen Boullosa
Leaving Tabasco
Grove Press, 2002

Jorge Comensal
The Mutations
Farrar, Straus and Giroux, 2019

Laura Esquivel
Like Water for Chocolate
Anchor, 1995, USA / Black Swan, 1993, UK

Yuri Herrera
Kingdom Cons
And Other Stories, 2017

Valeria Luiselli
The Story of My Teeth
Coffee House Press, 2015,
USA / Granta, 2016, UK

Fernanda Melchor
Hurricane Season
New Directions, 2020, USA /
Fitzcarraldo, 2022, UK

Élmer Mendoza
Name of the Dog
MacLehose, 2018

Emiliano Monge
What Goes Unsaid
Scribe, 2022

Silvia Moreno-Garcia
Mexican Gothic
Del Rey, 2020, USA /
Jo Fletcher Books, 2020, UK

Guadalupe Nettel
Still Born
Bloomsbury, 2023, USA /
Fitzcarraldo, 2022, UK

Elena Poniatowska
Tinisima
University of New Mexico Press, 2006

Paco Ignacio Taibo II
Four Hands
Restless Books (Kindle edition), 2015

NON-FICTION

Gloria Anzaldúa
Borderlands/La Frontera: The New Mestiza
Aunt Lute Books, 2022

Pino Cacucci
*The Whales Know: A Journey
Through Mexican California*
Haus, 2014

Francisco Cantú
The Line Becomes a River: Dispatches from the Mexican Border
Riverhead, 2019, USA / Vintage, 2019, UK

Katherine Corcoran
In the Mouth of the Wolf: A Murder, a Cover-Up, and the True Cost of Silencing the Press
Bloomsbury, 2022

Sandra Messinger Cypess
Uncivil Wars: Elena Garro, Octavio Paz, and the Battle for Cultural Memory
University of Texas Press, 2012

Caroline Dodds Pennock
On Savage Shores: How Indigenous Americans Discovered Europe
Knopf, 2023, USA / Orion, 2023, UK

Sergio González Rodríguez
The Femicide Machine
Semiotext(e), 2012

Tobin Hansen and María Engracia Robles Robles (eds)
Voices of the Border: Testimonios of Migration, Deportation, and Asylum
Georgetown University Press, 2021

Octavio Paz
The Labyrinth of Solitude
Penguin, 2005

Cristina Rivera Garza
Liliana's Invincible Summer: A Sister's Search for Justice
Hogarth, 2023, USA / Bloomsbury, 2023, UK

Camilla Townsend
Fifth Sun: A New History of the Aztecs
Oxford University Press, 2019

Juan Villoro
Horizontal Vertigo: A City Called Mexico
Pantheon, 2021

Javier Zamora
Solito: A Memoir
Hogarth, 2022, USA / Oneworld, 2022, UK

Oswaldo Zavala
Drug Cartels Do Not Exist: Narcotrafficking in US and Mexican Culture
Vanderbilt University Press, 2022

Graphic design and art direction: Tomo Tomo and Pietro Buffa

Photography: Fabio Cuttica
Photographic content curated by Prospekt Photographers

Illustrations: Edoardo Massa

Infographics and cartography: Propp

Managing editor (English-language edition): Simon Smith

Thanks to: Miguel Aguilar, Paula Canal, Nick Castro-Hernandez,
Michael Gaeb, Jacobo García, Victor Hurtado, Javier Lafuente,
María Lynch, Federico Mastrogiovanni, Emiliano Monge,
Marina Penalva, Lorenzo Ribaldi, José Luis Sanz, Nicole Witt.
Fabio Cuttica would like to thank his 'Tijuana family',
Espacio Migrante, Jessie Valcin, Wicky, Elana, José 'Pepe' Hernández,
Chely & Emiliano, Thalia Barrios, Norma Moreno, Reyna Aguilar,
Adriana Martínez, Gladys and Luigi, Agenzia Contrasto;
to Diana and Amalia for always being with me.

http://europaeditions.com/thepassenger
http://europaeditions.co.uk/thepassenger
#ThePassengerMag

The Passenger – Mexico
© Iperborea S.r.l., Milan, and Europa Editions, 2023

Translators: Italian — Oonagh Stransky ('The Pearl of the West',
'La Curandera'), Alan Thawley ('Final Stop: Tijuana', 'Mexico's Last
Four Presidents', 'Nuisance Neighbours', editorial, photographer's
biography, standfirsts, sidebars, captions); Spanish — Simon Deefholts
('Underground Tenochtitlan', 'An Author Recommends'), Kit Maude
('The Earth on Loan', 'The Forgotten Border of the Americas', 'Born There',
'The Playlist'), Kathryn Phillips-Miles ('A Woman Clothed with the
Sun', 'Stop that Train', 'A Girl All Alone by the Side of the Road'),
Sonia Verjovsky ('The Cocaine that Washes in from the Sea')

Translations © Iperborea S.r.l., Milan, and Europa Editions, 2023, except
'The Cocaine that Washes in from the Sea' © Sonia Verjovsky, 2021

ISBN 9781787704695

Printed on Munken Pure thanks to the support of Arctic
Paper Printed by ELCOGRAF S.p.A., Verona, Italy